P9-BXX-134

"FRAN LEBOWITZ is a writer. She is not a wise guy, not a dinner-party shortstop. Astringent, meticulous with language, Miss Lebowitz is a sort of Edwin Newman for the chic urban decay set....She wears life like an itchy muffler. She braids its fringes, flings it over her shoulder and savors its discomforts. ...METROPOLITAN LIFE is not simply consistently cross, swift and sly, as if that would not be enough. It introduces an important humorist in the classic tradition. The satire is principled, the taste impeccable—there is character here as well as personality. Miss Lebowitz has been doing a lot of writing. I want more."
—Jill Robinson, *New York Times Book Review*

"Nail transplants, specialty banking, digital clocks and pocket calculators, trendy clothes, mood jewelry—finding each one ridiculous in the extreme...Lebowitz is most perceptive when she surveys the New York scene; Los Angeles runs second in her crazy city sweepstakes."
—*Publishers Weekly*

"IF YOU ARE INCLINED TO VIEW THE PASSING SCENE WITH SOME ALARM, TAKE FRAN LEBOWITZ WITH YOU FOR COMIC RELIEF."
—*San Diego Union*

METROPOLITAN LIFE

METROPOLITAN LIFE

"A wonderful book...*METROPOLITAN LIFE* is strong stuff, with chapters designed to offend almost everyone.... But this is the era of gay bars and Erica Jong and 'parenting' and these blights demand powerful countermeasures. We have waited too long for a writer who is willing to point at her reader and warn: 'You are under arrest for being boring.' Truly the woman deserves a place of honor in a troubled time.... She should be treasured as an endangered species."

—Newsweek

"WRY, LIGHT AND LOVELY, NOT JUST FOR CITY FOLKS. SHE'S A CROSS BETWEEN ERMA BOMBECK AND S. J. PERELMAN. SHE'S SO GOOD, YOU HATE HER."

—US Magazine

"FRAN LEBOWITZ DOES FOR NEW YORK WHAT W. C. FIELDS DID FOR CHILDREN AND DOGS."

—Saturday Review

"FRAN LEBOWITZ's humor does not whine with neurosis or exploit race, creed and color; she doesn't sound like a stand-up comedian or like hand-me-down Woody Allen—all of which might explain why she can be both funny and a pleasure to read. At her best she is literate and imaginative, an intelligent writer in touch with the small insanities of life."

—Harper's

METROPOLITAN LIFE

"Try to imagine Jane Austen living in New York and writing a monthly column on the manners and mannerisms of the 1970s and you will have an idea of the appeal of FRAN LEBOWITZ....*METROPOLI-TAN LIFE* is paradise for the aphorism collector. Clothes with pictures and/or writing on them, discos, mood jewelry, landlords, music that does not know its place, houseplants, physical fitness, specialty banking, CB slang; all are targets for the deadly Lebowitz one-liner."

—*The Daily Texas*

"SPECTACULARLY FUNNY. ASTRINGENT, QUIETLY MISANTHROPIC, AND YET WISE FOR ALL HER DARK COMPLAINTS, LEBOWITZ WRITES WITH A SPARE AND LUCID PEN."

—*Washington Star*

"For those who rise and meet the day feeling less than friendly, help is now available. The prescription isn't harmful, although it can be habit-forming: just read a selection a day from Fran Lebowitz's hilarious METROPOLITAN LIFE and find an immediate cure for the break-of-the-day blues."

—*Associated Press*

Metropolitan Life

Fran Lebowitz

FAWCETT CREST • NEW YORK

A Fawcett Crest Book

Published by Ballantine Books

Copyright © 1974, 1975, 1976, 1977, 1978 by Fran
Lebowitz

ISBN 0-449-20089-2

This edition published by arrangement with Elsevier-
Dutton Publishing Company, Inc.

Selection of the Book-of-the-Month Club

Manufactured in the United States of America

First Fawcett Crest Edition: September 1979
First Ballantine Books Edition: July 1982

For my mother,
father and
sister

Contents

Most of these pieces appeared originally in Andy Warhol's *Interview* and in *Mademoiselle*. "MY DAY: An Introduction of Sorts" appeared in British *Vogue* in a slightly different form.

I would like to thank Laurie Colwin and Henry Robbins for their vocational guidance.

MY DAY: AN INTRODUCTION OF SORTS

12:35 P.M.—The phone rings. I am not amused. This is not my favorite way to wake up. My favorite way to wake up is to have a certain French movie star whisper to me softly at two-thirty in the afternoon that if I want to get to Sweden in time to pick up my Nobel Prize for Literature I had better ring for breakfast. This occurs rather less often than one might wish.

Today is a perfect example, for my caller is an agent from Los Angeles who informs me that I don't know him. True, and not without reason. He is audibly tan. He is interested in my work. His interest has led him to the conclusion that it would be a good idea for me to write a movie comedy. I would, of course, have total artistic freedom, for evidently comic writers have taken over the movie business. I look around my apartment (a feat readily accomplished by simply glancing up) and remark that Dino De Laurentiis would be surprised to hear that. He chuckles tanly and suggests that we talk. I suggest that we *are* talking. He, however, means *there* and at my own expense. I reply that the only way I could get to Los Angeles at my own expense is if I were to go by postcard. He chuckles again and suggests

12

that we talk. I agree to talk just as soon as I have won the Nobel Prize—for outstanding achievement in physics.

12:55 P.M.—I try to get back to sleep. Although sleeping is an area in which I have manifested an almost Algeresque grit and persistence, I fail to attain my goal.

1:20 P.M.—I go downstairs to get the mail. I get back into bed. Nine press releases, four screening notices, two bills, an invitation to a party in honor of a celebrated heroin addict, a final disconnect notice from New York Telephone, and three hate letters from *Mademoiselle* readers demanding to know just what it is that makes me think that I have the right to regard houseplants—*green, living* things—with such marked distaste. I call the phone company and try to make a deal, as actual payment is not a possibility. Would they like to go to a screening? Would they care to attend a party for a heroin addict? Are they interested in knowing just what it is that makes me think that I have the right to regard houseplants with such marked distaste? It seems they would not. They would like $148.10. I agree that this is, indeed, an understandable preference, but caution them against the bloodless quality of a life devoted to the blind pursuit of money. We are unable to reach a settlement. I pull up the covers and the phone rings. I spend the next few hours fending off editors, chatting amiably, and plotting revenge. I read. I smoke. The clock, unfortunately, catches my eye.

3:40 P.M.—I consider getting out of bed. I

reject the notion as being unduly vigorous. I read and smoke a bit more.

4:15 P.M.—I get up feeling curiously unrefreshed. I open the refrigerator. I decide against the half a lemon and jar of Gulden's mustard and on the spur of the moment choose instead to have breakfast out. I guess that's just the kind of girl I am—whimsical.

5:10 P.M.—I return to my apartment laden with magazines and spend the remainder of the afternoon reading arficles by writers who, regrettably, met their deadlines.

6:55 P.M.—A romantic interlude. The object of my affections arrives bearing a houseplant.

9:30 P.M.—I go to dinner with a group of people that includes two fashion models, a fashion photographer, a fashion photographer's representative, and an art director. I occupy myself almost entirely with the art director—drawn to him largely because he knows the most words.

2:05 A.M.—I enter my apartment and prepare to work. In deference to the slight chill I don two sweaters and an extra pair of socks. I pour myself a club soda and move the lamp next to the desk. I reread several old issues of *Rona Barrett's Hollywood* and a fair piece of *The Letters of Oscar Wilde*. I pick up my pen and stare at the paper. I light a cigarette. I stare at the paper. I write, "My Day: An Introduction of Sorts." Good. Lean yet cadenced. I consider my day. I become unaccountably depressed. I doodle in the margin. I jot down an idea I have for an all-black version of a Shakespearean comedy to be called *As You Likes It*. I look longingly at my sofa, not unmindful of the fact that it converts cleverly into a bed. I light a cigarette. I stare at the paper.

4:50 A.M.—The sofa wins. Another victory for furniture.

MANNERS

I am not a callous sort. I believe that all people should have warm clothing, sufficient food, and adequate shelter. I do feel, however, that unless they are willing to behave in an acceptable manner they should bundle up, chow down, and stay home.

I speak here not only of etiquette, for while etiquette is surely a factor, acceptable behavior is comprised of a good deal more. It demands, for instance, that the general public refrain from starting trends, overcoming inhibitions, or developing hidden talents. It further requires acceptance of the fact that the common good is usually not very and that there is indeed such a thing as getting carried away with democracy. Oppression and/or repression are not without their charms nor freedom and/or license their drawbacks. This can clearly be seen in the following chart.

THE BY-PRODUCTS OF OPPRESSION AND/OR REPRESSION	THE BY-PRODUCTS OF FREEDOM AND/OR LICENSE

WOMEN

1. Well-kept fingernails

2. Homemade cookies

3. A guarantee that at least one segment of the population could be relied upon to display a marked distaste for strenuous physical activity

4. The distinct probability that even a small gathering would yield at least one person who knew how to respond properly to a wedding invitation

5. Real coffee

1. The word *chairperson*

2. The acceptance of construction boots as suitable attire for members of the fair sex

3. Girl ministers

4. The male centerfold

5. Erica Jong

JEWS

1. Highly entertaining stand-up comedians

2. The Stage Delicatessen

1. Progressive nursery schools

2. Frozen bagels

3. A guarantee that at least one segment of the population could be relied upon to display a marked distaste for strenuous physical activity

3. The Upper West Side

4. The development and perfection of theatrical law as a flourishing profession

4. The notion that it is appropriate for a writer to surrender a percentage of his income to an agent

5. Interesting slang expressions, particularly those used to describe Gentiles

5. Erica Jong

BLACKS

1. Jazz

1. Strawberry wine

2. The provision of the southern portion of the United States with a topic of conversation

2. Negro accountants

3. Tap dancing

3. Inventive forms of handshaking

4. The preservation in our culture of a lively interest in revenge

4. Open admissions

5. Amos 'n' Andy

5. Sammy Davis, Jr.

6. Interesting slang expressions, particularly those used to describe white people

6. The Symbionese Liberation Army

TEEN-AGERS

1. The thrill of illicit drinking

1. Strawberry wine

2. Sexual denial and the resultant development of truly exciting sexual fantasies

2. Easy sexual access and the resultant premature boredom

3. The swank of juvenile delinquency

3. Social commitment

4. The glamour of alienation

4. People who may very well just be discovering symbolist poetry being allowed to vote

HOMOSEXUALS

1. Precision theatrical dancing

1. *A Chorus Line*

2. Sarcasm

2. Amyl nitrite

3. Art

3. Leather underwear

4. Literature

4. Lesbian mothers

5. Real gossip

5. Heterosexual hair-
dressers

6. The amusing notion
that *Who's Afraid of
Virginia Woolf* was real-
ly about two men

6. The amusing notion
that *Who's Afraid of
Virginia Woolf* was real-
ly about a man and a
woman

Two basic steps must be taken in order to
reach the eventual goal of acceptable behavior.
The first (which I assume you have already
accomplished) is a careful perusal of the above
chart. The second is ridding oneself of certain
popular and harmful misconceptions, as follows:

It is not true that there is dignity in all work.
Some jobs are definitely better than others. It is
not hard to tell the good jobs from the bad. People
who have good jobs are happy, rich, and well
dressed. People who have bad jobs are unhappy,
poor and use meat extenders. Those who seek
dignity in the type of work that compels them to
help hamburgers are certain to be disappointed.
Also to be behaving badly.

There is no such thing as inner peace. There is
only nervousness or death. Any attempt to prove
otherwise constitutes unacceptable behavior.

Very few people possess true artistic ability. It
is therefore both unseemly and unproductive to
irritate the situation by making an effort. If you
have a burning, restless urge to write or paint,

simply eat something sweet and the feeling will pass. Your life story would not make a good book. Do not even try.

All God's children are not beautiful. Most of God's children are, in fact, barely presentable. The most common error made in matters of appearance is the belief that one should disdain the superficial and let the true beauty of one's soul shine through. If there are places on your body where this is a possibility, you are not attractive—you are leaking.

Vocational Guidance for the Truly Ambitious

People of every age are interested in bettering themselves. It is with this in mind that the majority choose their life work. Most professions require specific training and skills. Some, however—those a bit off the beaten track—must be entered in a different fashion. Since these fields are often the most difficult to gain a foothold in, one is advised to make certain that one is really suited to this type of work. It is with this in mind that I offer the following series of tests.

So You Want to Be the Pope?

This position has traditionally been reserved for men. Women interested in this job should be warned of the almost insurmountable odds against them. Religion also plays an important role here, so if you have your doubts you would be well advised to consider something a touch less restrictive.

1. I most enjoy speaking...
   a. On the phone.
   b. After dinner.
   c. Off the cuff.
   d. In private.
   e. Ex cathedra.
2. Of the following, my favorite name is...
   a. Muffy.
   b. Vito.
   c. Ira.
   d. Jim Bob.
   e. Innocent XIII.
3. Most of my friends are...
   a. Left-wing intellectuals.
   b. Loose women.
   c. Quality people.
   d. Regular guys.
   e. Good sports.
   f. Cardinals.
4. All roads lead to...
   a. Bridgehampton.
   b. Cap d'Antibes.
   c. Midtown.
   d. Tampa.
   e. Rome.
5. Complete this phrase or word. Dog...
   a. House.
   b. Food.
   c. Tired.
   d. Days.
   e. ma.
6. My friends call me...
   a. Stretch.
   b. Doc.
   c. Toni.
   d. Izzy.
   e. Supreme Pontiff.
7. For dress-up occasions I prefer...
   a. Something kicky yet elegant.

  b. Anything by Halston.
  c. Evening pajamas.
  d. A surplice and miter.
8. I would feel most secure knowing that I had...
  a. Enough money.
  b. A good alarm system.
  c. A big dog.
  d. A union contract.
  e. The Swiss Guard.
9. When annoyed at myself for taking it too easy I...
  a. Go on a low-carbohydrate diet.
  b. Read Emerson.
  c. Swim forty laps.
  d. Chop firewood.
  e. Wash the feet of the poor.

So You Want to Be an Heiress?

This is a field in which accident of birth carries a lot of weight. One can overcome the problem by marrying well and/or making an old man very happy. Such a method is, however, by no means easy and the lazy would do well to seek employment elsewhere.

1. If I had to describe myself in just one word, that word would be...
  a. Kindly.
  b. Energetic.
  c. Curious.
  d. Pleasant.
  e. Madcap.

2. I cross...
   a. Only after looking both ways.
   b. Town by bus.
   c. The days off the calendar.
   d. My sevens.
3. On weekends I like to go...
   a. Camping.
   b. Roller skating.
   c. For long walks.
   d. Bar hopping.
   e. To Gstaad.
4. I find that a good way to break the ice with people is to ask them where they...
   a. Buy their vegetables.
   b. Shop for appliances.
   c. Get their pictures developed.
   d. Winter.
5. Poppy is...
   a. A red flower.
   b. Heroin in the raw.
   c. A type of seed that appears occasionally in bread and rolls.
   d. My nickname.
6. Men make the best...
   a. Fried chicken.
   b. Flower arrangements.
   c. Drinks.
   d. Valets.
7. As a small child I liked to play...
   a. Dolls.
   b. Doctor.
   c. Baseball.
   d. Candyland.
   e. Mansion.
8. I never carry...
   a. A briefcase.
   b. Tales.
   c. Typhoid.
   d. Cash.

9. My first big crush was on...
   a. Tab Hunter.
   b. Paul McCartney.
   c. The boy next door.
   d. My horse.

So You Want to Be an Absolute Political Dictator?

This job requires stamina, drive, and an iron will. Not recommended for the shy type.

1. My greatest fear is...
   a. Meeting new people.
   b. Heights.
   c. Snakes.
   d. The dark.
   e. A coup d'etat.
2. On a lazy Sunday afternoon I most enjoy...
   a. Cooking.
   b. Experimenting with makeup.
   c. Going to a museum.
   d. Just lounging around the house.
   e. Exiling people.
3. I think people look best in...
   a. Formal attire.
   b. Bathing suits.
   c. Clothes that reflect their life-style.
   d. Bermuda shorts.
   e. Prison uniforms.
4. When confronted by a large crowd of strangers my immediate reaction is to...
   a. Introduce myself to anyone who looks interesting.
   b. Wait for them to speak to me first.
   c. Sit in a corner and sulk.
   d. Start a purge.

5. The proper manner in which to respond to a chance meeting with me is by . . .
   a. Smiling.
   b. Nodding.
   c. Saying hello.
   d. Giving me a little kiss.
   e. Saluting.
6. When someone disagrees with me my first instinct is to . . .
   a. Try to understand his point of view.
   b. Get into a pet.
   c. Discuss it calmly and rationally.
   d. Cry.
   e. Have him executed.
7. Nothing builds character like . . .
   a. Scouting.
   b. The YMCA.
   c. Sunday school.
   d. Cold showers.
   e. Forced labor.

So You Want to Be a Social Climber?

Of all the occupations dealt with here, this is undoubtedly the easiest to crack. It is also, alas, the hardest to stomach—a fact that seems to have had surprisingly little effect upon the hordes that crowd the field.

1. When alone I most often . . .
   a. Read.
   b. Watch television.
   c. Write sonnets.
   d. Build model planes.
   e. Call the Beverly Hills Hotel and have myself paged.

2. Were a female friend to say something particularly amusing I would most likely...
   a. Say, "Hey, that was really funny."
   b. Laugh delightedly.
   c. Giggle uncontrollably.
   d. Say, "You're so like Dottie."

3. When the phone rings I am most likely to answer by saying...
   a. "Hello, how are you?"
   b. "Oh, hello."
   c. "Hi."
   d. "Oh, hi, I was just listening to one of Wolfgang's little symphonies."

4. If my house or apartment was on fire the first thing I would save would be...
   a. My son.
   b. My cat.
   c. My boyfriend.
   d. My mention in *Women's Wear Daily*.

5. I consider dining out to be...
   a. A pleasure.
   b. A nice change.
   c. An opportunity to see friends.
   d. A romantic interlude.
   e. A career.

6. My idea of a good party is...
   a. A big, noisy bash, with lots of liquor and lots of action.
   b. Good talk, good food, good wine.
   c. A few close friends for dinner and bridge.
   d. One to which I cannot get invited.

7. If I were stranded alone on a desert island and could have only one book I would want...
   a. The Bible.
   b. The Complete Works of William Shakespeare.
   c. *The Wind in the Willows.*
   d. Truman Capote's address book.

8. Some of my best friends are ...
   a. Jewish.
   b. Negro.
   c. Puerto Rican.
   d. Unaware of my existence.
9. As far as I am concerned, a rose by any other name is ...
   a. Still the same.
   b. A flower.
   c. A color.
   d. A scent.
   e. A Kennedy.

So You Want to Be an Empress?

Once again we are confronted with the problem of family connections. Do not be deceived, however, by this job's apparent similarity to the heiress game, for it requires a good deal more responsibility. You would be a very foolish girl, though, were you to let that discourage you, for this is the only sort of work that offers the richly rewarding satisfactions of being served by others.

1. Complete the following phrase: Ladies ...
   a. Room.
   b. Lunch.
   c. Watches.
   d. First.
   e. -in-waiting.
2. My pet peeve about my husband is his ...
   a. Snoring.
   b. Habit of leaving the cap off the toothpaste.
   c. Drinking buddies.

    d. Stubbornness.

    e. Imperial concubines.

3. I simply don't know what I'd do without my...

    a. WaterPik.

    b. Answering service.

    c. Mr. Coffee.

    d. Official taster.

4. I think that the best way to get ahead in the world is by...

    a. Hard work.

    b. Good connections.

    c. Playing fair.

    d. Going to a decent college.

    e. Divine right.

5. I always wanted my mother to be...

    a. More liberal.

    b. Less nosy.

    c. A better cook.

    d. Young at heart.

    e. Empress dowager.

6. I think people should stand on...

    a. Principle.

    b. Firm ground.

    c. Their own two feet.

    d. Tiptoe.

    e. Ceremony.

7. I feel that it is most important to establish...

    a. Rapport.

    b. A decent working relationship.

    c. A precedent.

    d. A dynasty.

8. The best things in life are...

    a. Free.

    b. Slaves.

9. I would most like to spend Christmas in...

    a. Connecticut.

    b. Palm Beach.

    c. Great Gorge.

    d. The Winter Palace.
10. I think men are at their most attractive when...
    a. Playing tennis.
    b. Sleeping.
    c. Dancing.
    d. Laughing.
    e. Kneeling.
11. If I could afford an addition to my house I would build...
    a. A workshop.
    b. A den.
    c. A patio.
    d. A sauna.
    e. A throne room.
12. I would most like my son to be...
    a. Neat.
    b. A chip off the old block.
    c. A doctor.
    d. Good at sports.
    e. Crown prince.
13. On a date I most enjoy...
    a. An art film.
    b. Bowling.
    c. Dinner and the theater.
    d. Ruling.

Modern Sports

When it comes to sports I am not particularly interested. Generally speaking, I look upon them as dangerous and tiring activities performed by people with whom I share nothing except the right to trial by jury. It is not that I am totally indifferent to the joys of athletic effort—it is simply that my idea of what constitutes sport does not coincide with popularly held notions on the subject. There are a number of reasons for this, chief among them being that to me the outdoors is what you must pass through in order to get from your apartment into a taxicab.

There *are*, however, several contests in which I *do* engage and not, I might add, without a certain degree of competence. The following is by no means a complete list:

1. Ordering in Some Breakfast.
2. Picking Up the Mail.
3. Going Out for Cigarettes.
4. Meeting for a Drink.

As you can see, these are largely urban activities and, as such, not ordinarily regarded with much respect by sports enthusiasts. Nevertheless, they all require skill, stamina, and courage. And they all have their penalties and their rewards.

There are many such activities and I, for one, feel that the time is ripe for them to receive proper recognition. I therefore propose that those in charge of the 1980 Olympic Games invite New York to participate as a separate entity. The New York team would be entered in only one contest, to be called the New York Decathlon. The New York Decathlon would consist of four events instead of the usual ten, since everyone in New York is very busy. It would further differ from the conventional decathlon in that each contestant would enter only one event, since in New York it pays to specialize. The four events would be Press Agentry, Dry Cleaning and Laundering, Party-going, and Dog-owning.

Traditionally the Olympic Games open with a torch-bearer followed by all the athletes marching around the stadium carrying flags. This will not be changed, but in 1980 the athletes will be followed by seventeen Checker cabs carrying the New York team. The first cabby in line will have his arm out the window and in his hand will be a torch. The passengers in this cab will be screaming at the cabby as sparks fly into the back seat. He will pretend not to hear them. When the parade concludes, the first cabby will fail to notice this immediately and he will be compelled to stop short. This will cause all the following cabs to run into each other. The cabbies will then spend the rest of the Olympics yelling at each other and

writing things down in a threatening manner.
The athletics teams will be forced to start the
games even though this collision has occurred
where it will cause the greatest inconvenience.

Press Agentry

The two contestants enter the stadium from
opposite sides, having first been assured by the
referee that both sides are equally important.
They kiss each other on both cheeks and turn
smartly toward the crowd. They do not look past
the first ten rows. They then seat themselves on
facing Ultrasuede sofas and light cigarettes. Two
moonlighting ball boys race in with coffee black,
no sugar. The contestants pick up their ringing
phones. Points awarded as follows:

1. For not taking the most calls from people
   who wish to speak to you.
2. For waking up the most people who do not.
3. For telling the most people who want to
   attend an event that they can't have tickets.
4. For telling the most people who do not want
   to attend said event that you have already
   sent them tickets by messenger and that
   they owe you a favor.

Dry Cleaning and Laundering

Two fully equipped dry cleaning and laundering establishments are constructed in inconven-

ient areas of the stadium. Several innocent people enter each establishment. These people serve the same function in this event that the fox serves in a hunt. They place upon the counters piles of soiled clothing, receive little slips of colored paper, and leave. Points awarded as follows:

1. For ripping off the most buttons.
   a. Additional points if buttons are impossible to replace.
2. For washing the most silk shirts bearing labels stating DRY CLEAN ONLY.
   a. Additional points if shirts are washed with bleeding madras jackets.
   b. If shirts are white, victory is near.
3. For boxing the most shirts requested on hangers.
4. For losing the most garments.
   a. Additional points according to expensiveness of garments.
5. For being the most ingenious in moving ink spots from one pant leg to the other.

Party-going

A room exactly half the size necessary is built in the center of the stadium. Too many contestants enter the room. Points awarded as follows:

1. For getting to the bar.
2. For getting away from the bar.
3. For accidentally spilling wine on an opponent to whom you have lost a job.

4. For inadvertently dropping a hot cigarette ash on same.
5. For making the greatest number of funny remarks about people not present.
6. For arriving the latest with the greatest number of famous people.
7. For leaving the earliest with an old lover's new flame.

Dog-owning

There has been erected in the stadium an exact replica of a fifteen-block section of Greenwich Village. Twenty contestants leave buildings on the perimeter of this area, each walking three dogs who have not been out of the house all day. The object of the game is to be the first to get to the sidewalk directly in front of my building.

When all of the points are added up, the contestant with the greatest number of points enters the stadium. He is followed by the two contestants with the next greatest number of points. The two runners-up go off to one side with the referee. The referee takes out a stopwatch. Each runner-up has five minutes in which to explain in an entertaining manner why *he* did not receive the most points. Whichever runner-up is the more arrogant and convincing is presented with the gold medal. Because in New York it's not whether you win or lose—it's how you lay the blame.

Breeding Will Tell:
A Family Treatment

There once appeared in a magazine a photograph of myself taken under obviously youthful circumstances. I assumed that it would be readily apparent to all that this was my high school yearbook picture. I neglected, however, to take into consideration that I number among my acquaintances some people of decidedly lofty background. I was first jarred into awareness of this by a well-born young fashion model who, in reference to said photograph, offered, "I really loved your deb picture, Fran." Had that been the end of it I would undoubtedly have forgotten the incident, but later on that very same evening an almost identical remark was made by a minor member of the Boston aristocracy. As far as I was concerned this constituted a trend. I therefore felt faced with a decision: either snort derisively at the very idea or create an amusing fiction appropriate to such thinking. Being at least peripherally in the amusing fiction business, I chose the latter and thus have prepared the following genealogy.

Margaret Lebovitz, my paternal grandmother, was born in Ghetto Point, Hungary (a restricted community), at the very dawn of the Gay Nineties. An appealing child, she was often left in

the care of trusted family retainers (my Aunt
Sadie and Uncle Benny), as her father's far-flung
business affairs—which were mainly concerned
with being conscripted into the army—
frequently kept him away from home. Although
her mother spent most of her time amusing
herself in the cabbage fields, she nevertheless
made it a point to visit the nursery every evening
and stand guard while little Margaret said her
prayers. Margaret's childhood was a happy one—
she and her chums exchanged confidences and
babushkas as they whiled away the carefree
hours picking beets and playing hide and seek
with the Cossacks. Tariff, the family estate,
where the Lebovitzes wintered (*and* summered)
was indeed a wondrous place and it was therefore
not surprising when Margaret balked at being
sent away to school. Her father, home on a brief
desertion, took her into his straw-lined study—
which was affectionately called "Daddy's
hideout"—and explained patiently that unbreak-
able tradition demanded that girls of Margaret's
class acquire the necessary social graces such as
fleeing demurely and staying properly alive.
Margaret listened respectfully and agreed to
begin her freshman year at Miss Belief's.

Margaret was a great success at Miss Belief's,
where her taste in footwear quickly won her the
nickname Bootsie. Bootsie was an excellent
student and demonstrated such a flair for barely
audible breathing that she was unanimously
elected chairman of the Spring Day Escape
Committee. That is not to say that Bootsie was a

grind—quite the contrary. An irrepressible madcap, Bootsie got herself into such bad scrapes that the fellow members of her club, the Huddled Masses, were frequently compelled to come to her rescue. Fond of outdoor sports, Bootsie longed for summer vacation and happily joined in the girlish cries of "Serf's up!" that greeted the season.

Upon reaching her eighteenth birthday, Bootsie made her debut into society and her beauty, charm, and way with a hoe soon gained her a reputation as the Brenda Frazier of Ghetto Point. All of the young men in her set were smitten with Bootsie and found it absolutely necessary to secure the promise of a waltz days in advance of a party, as her dance pogrom was invariably full. Bootsie's favorite beau was Tibor, a tall, dashing young deserter and two-time winner of the Hungarian Cup Race, which was held yearly in a lavishly irrigated wheat field. Tibor was fond of Bootsie, but he was not unmindful of the fact that she would one day come into her father's great plowshare, and this was his primary interest in her. The discovery that Tibor was a fortune hunter had a devastating effect upon Bootsie and she took to her bed. Bootsie's family, understandably concerned about her condition, held a meeting to discuss the problem. It was concluded that a change of scenery would do her a world of good. A plan of action was decided upon and thus Bootsie Lebovitz was sent steerage to Ellis Island in order that she might forget.

Disco Hints:
The New Etiquette

It may come as somewhat of a surprise to those who know me only as a woman of letters to learn that I am quite fond of dancing and not half bad at it either. I am not, however, fond of large groups of people. This is unfortunate, for it is not feasible to bring into one's own home all of the desirable accoutrements of discothèque dancing such as a deejay, several hours of tape, and the possibility, slim as it might be, of meeting one's own true love. I am therefore compelled to spend night after night amongst hordes of strangers, many of whom conduct themselves without the slightest regard for the sensibilities of their fellow dancers. This has led me to compile a short list of helpful tips to ensure more pleasant dancing for all.

1. When the discothèque in question is a private club with a strict members-only policy, it is not good form to stand outside and beg in an unattractive tone of voice to be taken in. It is even less appealing to threaten the life or reputation of an entering member with either a knife or the information that you know his real name and are planning on phoning his hometown newspaper with the true reason why he hasn't married.

2. There is no question but that after a few moments of dancing you are likely to become quite warm. This should not be taken as a cue to remove your shirt. If one of your fellow dancers should be interested in your progress at the gym, rest assured that he will not be too shy to ask. Should you find the heat unbearable you can just take that bandanna out of your back pocket and blot your forehead. Just be sure you put it back on the right side.

3. If you are of the opinion that an evening without amyl nitrite is like a day without sunshine, you should avail yourself of this substance in the privacy of your own truck and not in the middle of a crowded dance floor.

4. If you are a disc jockey, kindly remember that your job is to play records that people will enjoy dancing to and not to impress possible visiting disc jockeys with your esoteric taste. People generally enjoy dancing to songs that have words and are of a reasonable length. Sixteen-minute instrumentals by West African tribal drummers are frequently the cause of undue amyl nitrite consumption and shirt removal.

Better Read Than Dead:
A Revised Opinion

My attendance at grammar school coincided rather unappealingly with the height of the cold war. This resulted in my spending a portion of each day sitting cross-legged, head in lap, either alone under my desk or, more sociably, against the wall in the corridor. When not so occupied I could be found sitting in class reading avidly about the horrors of life under Communism. I was not a slow child, but I believed passionately that Communists were a race of horned men who divided their time equally between the burning of Nancy Drew books and the devising of a plan of nuclear attack that would land the largest and most lethal bomb squarely upon the third-grade class of Thomas Jefferson School in Morristown, New Jersey. This was a belief widely held among my classmates and it was reinforced daily by teachers and those parents who were of the Republican persuasion.

Among the many devices used to keep this belief alive was a detailed chart that appeared yearly in our social studies book. This chart pointed out the severe economic hardships of Communist life. The reading aloud of the chart was accompanied by a running commentary from the teacher and went something like this:

"This chart shows how long a man must work in Russia in order to purchase the following goods. We then compare this to the length of time it takes a man in the United States to earn enough money to purchase the same goods."

RUSSIA   U.S.A.

A PAIR OF SHOES—38 HOURS

A PAIR OF SHOES—2 HOURS

"And they only have brown oxfords in Russia, so that nobody ever gets to wear shoes without straps even for dress-up. Also they have never even heard of Capezios, and if they did, no one would be allowed to wear them because they all have to work on farms whenever they are not busy making atom bombs."

"And we have all kinds of shoes, even Pappagallos."

A LOAF OF BREAD—2½ HOURS

A LOAF OF BREAD—5 MINUTES

"They do not have peanut butter in Russia, or Marshmallow Fluff, and their bread has a lot of crust on it, which they force all the children to eat."

"We have cinnamon raisin bread and english muffins and we can put whatever we like on it because we have democracy."

A POUND OF NAILS—6 HOURS

"And they need a lot of nails in Russia because everyone has to work very hard all the time building things—even mothers."

A POUND OF NAILS—8 MINUTES

"Even though we don't need that many nails because we have Scotch tape and staples."

A STATION WAGON—9 YEARS

"If they were even permitted to own them, which they are not, so everyone has to walk everywhere even though they are very tired from building so many things like atom bombs."

A STATION WAGON—4 MONTHS

"And we have so many varieties to choose from—some painted to look like wood on the side and some that are two different colors. We also have lots of other cars, such as convertible sports cars."

A PAIR OF OVERALLS—11 HOURS

"And everyone has to wear overalls all the time and they're all the same color so nobody gets to wear straight skirts even if they're in high school."

A PAIR OF OVERALLS—1 HOUR

"But since we can choose what we want to wear in a democracy, most farmers wear overalls and they like to wear them."

A DOZEN EGGS—7 HOURS

"But they hardly ever get to eat them because eggs are a luxury in Russia and there are no luxuries under Communism."

A DOZEN EGGS—9 MINUTES

"We have lots of eggs here and that is why we can have eggnog, egg salad, even Easter eggs, except for the Jewish children in the class, who

A TELEVISION SET—2 YEARS

"But they don't have them. That's right, they do not have TV in Russia because they know that if the people in Russia were allowed to watch *Leave It to Beaver* they would all want to move to the United States, and probably most of them would want to come to Morristown."

I'm sure have something just as nice on their holiday, which is called Hanukkah."

A TELEVISION SET—2 WEEKS

"And many people have two television sets and some people like Dougie Bershey have color TV so that he can tell everyone in class what color everything was on *Walt Disney*."

All of this was duly noted by both myself and my classmates, and the vast majority of us were rather right-wing all through grammar school. Upon reaching adolescence, however, a number of us rebelled and I must admit to distinctly leftist leanings during my teen years. Little by little, though, I have been coming around to my former way of thinking and, while I am not all that enamored of our local form of government, I have reacquired a marked distaste for Theirs.

My political position is based largely on my aversion to groups, and if there's one thing I know about Communism it's that large groups are definitely in the picture. I do not work well with others and I do not wish to learn to do so. I do not even dance well with others if there are too many of them, and I have no doubt but that Communist discothèques are hideously over-crowded. "From each according to his ability, to each according to his needs" is not a decision I care to leave to politicians, for I do not believe that an ability to remark humorously on the passing scene would carry much weight with one's comrades or that one could convince them of the need for a really reliable answering service. The common good is not my cup of tea—it is the uncommon good in which I am interested, and I do not deceive myself that such statements are much admired by the members of farming collectives. Communists all seem to wear small caps, a look I consider better suited to tubes of toothpaste than to people. We number, of course, among us our own cap wearers, but I assure you they are easily avoided. It is my understanding that Communism requires of its adherents that they arise early and participate in a strenuous round of calisthenics. To someone who wishes that cigarettes came already lit the thought of such exertion at any hour when decent people are just nodding off is thoroughly abhorrent. I have been further advised that in the Communist world an aptitude for speaking or writing in an amusing fashion doesn't count for spit. I therefore have every intention of doing my best to keep the Iron Curtain from being drawn across Fifty-seventh Street. It is to this end that I have prepared a little chart of my own for the edification of my fellow New Yorkers.

The following chart compares the amount of time it takes a Communist to earn enough to purchase the following goods against the amount of time it takes a New Yorker to do the same.

COMMUNIST	NEW YORKER
A CO-OP APARTMENT IN THE EAST SEVENTIES ON THE PARK—4,000 YEARS. And even then you have to share it with the rest of the collective. There is not a co-op in the city with that many bathrooms.	A CO-OP APARTMENT IN THE EAST SEVENTIES ON THE PARK—No time at all if you were lucky in the parent department. If you have not been so blessed it could take as long as twenty years, but at least you'd have your own bathroom.
A SUBSCRIPTION TO *The New Yorker*—3 WEEKS. And even then it is doubtful that you'd understand the cartoons.	A SUBSCRIPTION TO *The New Yorker*—1 HOUR, maybe less, because in a democracy one frequently receives such things as gifts.
A FIRST-CLASS AIRPLANE TICKET TO PARIS—6 MONTHS—Paris, Comrade? Not so fast.	A FIRST-CLASS AIRPLANE TICKET TO PARIS—Varies widely, but any smart girl can acquire such a ticket with ease if she plays her cards right.
A FERNANDO SANCHEZ NIGHTGOWN—	A FERNANDO SANCHEZ NIGHTGOWN—

3 MONTHS. With the cap. Very attractive.

1 WEEK, less if you know someone in the business, and need I point out that your chances of being so connected are far greater in a democracy such as ours than they are in Peking.

DINNER AT A FINE RESTAURANT — 2 YEARS to earn the money; 27 years for the collective to decide on a restaurant.

DINNER AT A FINE RESTAURANT — No problem if one has chosen one's friends wisely.

Children: Pro or Con?

Moving, as I do, in what would kindly be called artistic circles, children are an infrequent occurrence. But even the most artistic of circles includes within its periphery a limited edition of the tenaciously domestic.

As I am generally quite fond of children I accept this condition with far less displeasure than do my more rarefied acquaintances. That is not to imply that I am a total fool for a little grin but simply that I consider myself to be in a position of unquestionable objectivity and therefore eminently qualified to deal with the subject in an authoritative manner.

From the number of children in evidence it appears that people have them at the drop of a hat—for surely were they to give this matter its due attention they would act with greater decorum. Of course, until now prospective parents have not had the opportunity to see the facts spelled out in black and white and therefore cannot reasonably be held accountable for their actions. To this end I have carefully set down all pertinent information in the fervent hope that it will result in a future populated by a more attractive array of children than I have thus far encountered.

Pro

I must take issue with the term "a mere child," for it has been my invariable experience that the company of a mere child is infinitely preferable to that of a mere adult.

* * *

Children are usually small in stature, which makes them quite useful for getting at those hard-to-reach places.

* * *

Children do not sit next to one in restaurants and discuss their preposterous hopes for the future in loud tones of voice.

* * *

Children ask better questions than do adults. "May I have a cookie?" "Why is the sky blue?" and "What does a cow say?" are far more likely to elicit a cheerful response than "Where's your manuscript?" "Why haven't you called?" and "Who's your lawyer?"

* * *

Children give life to the concept of immaturity.

* * *

Children make the most desirable opponents in Scrabble as they are both easy to beat and fun to cheat.

* * *

It is still quite possible to stand in a throng of children without once detecting even the faintest whiff of an exciting, rugged after-shave or cologne.

* * *

Not a single member of the under-age set has yet to propose the word *chairchild*.

* * *

Children sleep either alone or with small toy animals. The wisdom of such behavior is unquestionable, as it frees them from the immeasurable tedium of being privy to the whispered confessions of others. I have yet to run across a teddy bear who was harboring the secret desire to wear a maid's uniform.

Con

Even when freshly washed and relieved of all obvious confections, children tend to be sticky. One can only assume that this has something to do with not smoking enough.

* * *

Children have decidedly little fashion sense and if left to their own devices will more often than not be drawn to garments of unfortunate cut. In this respect they do not differ greatly from the majority of their elders, but somehow one blames them more.

* * *

Children respond inadequately to sardonic humor and veiled threats.

* * *

Notoriously insensitive to subtle shifts in mood, children will persist in discussing the color of a recently sighted cement-mixer long after one's own interest in the topic has waned.

* * *

Children are rarely in the position to lend one a truly interesting sum of money. There are, however, exceptions, and such children are an excellent addition to any party.

* * *

Children arise at an unseemly hour and are ofttimes in the habit of putting food on an empty stomach.

* * *

Children do not look well in evening clothes.

* * *

All too often children are accompanied by adults.

A Manual:
Training for Landlords

Every profession requires of its members certain skills, talents, or training. Dancers must be light on their feet. Brain surgeons must attend medical school. Candlestick-makers must have an affinity for wax. These occupations, though, are only the tip of the iceberg. How do others learn their trades? We shall see.

How to Be a Landlord: An Introduction

In order to be a landlord, it is first necessary to acquire a building or buildings. This can be accomplished in either of two ways. By far the most pleasant is by means of inheritance—a method favored not only because it is easy on the pocketbook but also because it eliminates the tedious chore of selecting the property. This manual, however, is not really intended for landlords of that stripe, since such an inheritance invariably includes a genetic composition that makes formal instruction quite superfluous.

Less attractive but somewhat more common (how often those traits go hand in hand) is the method of actual purchase. And it is here that our work really begins.

Lesson One: Buying

Buildings can be divided into two main groups: cheap and expensive. It should be remembered, however, that these terms are for professional use only and never to be employed in the presence of tenants, who, almost without exception, prefer the words *very* and *reasonable*. If the price of a building strikes you as excessive, you would do well to consider that wise old slogan "It's not the initial cost—it's the upkeep," for as landlord you are in the enviable position of having entered a profession in which the upkeep is taken care of by the customer. This concept may be somewhat easier to grasp by simply thinking of yourself as a kind of telephone company. You will be further encouraged when you realize that while there may indeed be a wide disparity in building prices, this terrible inequity need not be passed on to the tenant in the degrading form of lower rent. It should now be clear to the attentive student that choosing a building is basically a matter of personal taste and, since it is the rare landlord who is troubled by such a quality, we shall proceed to the next lesson.

Lesson Two: Rooms

The most important factor here is that you understand that a room is a matter of opinion. It is, after all, your building, and if you choose to designate a given amount of space as a room, then indeed it *is* a room. Specifying the function of the room is also your responsibility, and tenants need frequently to be reminded of this as they will all too often display a tendency to call one of your rooms a closet. This is, of course, a laughable pretension, since few tenants have ever seen a closet.

Lesson Three: Walls

A certain number of walls are one of the necessary evils of the business. And while some of you will understandably bridle at the expense, the observant student is aware that walls offer a good return on investment by way of providing one of the basic components of rooms. That is not to say that you, as landlord, must be a slave to convention. Plaster and similarly substantial materials are embarrassingly passé to the progressive student. If you are a father, you know that walls can enjoyably be made by children at home or camp with a simple paste of flour and water and some of Daddy's old newspapers. The childless landlord might well be interested in Wallies—a valuable new product that comes on a roll. Wallies tear off easily and *can* be painted, should such a procedure ever be enforced by law.

Lesson Four: Heat

The arrival of winter seems invariably to infect
the tenant with an almost fanatical lust for
warmth. Sweaters and socks he may have galore;
yet he refuses to perceive their usefulness and
stubbornly and selfishly insists upon obtaining
his warmth through *your* heat. There are any
number of ploys available to the resourceful
landlord, but the most effective requires an
actual cash outlay. No mind, it's well worth it—
fun, too. Purchase a tape recorder. Bring the tape
recorder to your suburban home and place it in
the vicinity of your heater. Here its sensitive
mechanism will pick up the sounds of impending
warmth. This recording played at high volume in
the basement of the building has been known to
stymie tenants for days on end.

Lesson Five: Water

It is, of course, difficult for the landlord to
understand the tenant's craving for water when
the modern supermarket is fairly bursting with
juices and soft drinks of every description. The
burden is made no easier by the fact that at least
some of the time this water must be hot. The
difficult situation is only partially alleviated by
the knowledge that *hot*, like *room*, is a matter of
opinion.

Lesson Six: Roaches

It is the solemn duty of every landlord to maintain an adequate supply of roaches. The minimum acceptable roach to tenant ratio is four thousand to one. Should this arrangement prompt an expression of displeasure on the part of the tenant, ignore him absolutely. The tenant is a notorious complainer. Just why this is so is not certain, though a number of theories abound. The most plausible of these ascribes the tenant's chronic irritability to his widely suspected habit of drinking enormous quantities of heat and hot water—a practice well known to result in the tragically premature demise of hallway light bulbs.

Success Without College

The term *stage mother* is used to describe a female parent who, to put it kindly, has taken it upon herself to instill in her child theatrical ambition and eventual success. The entire upbringing of the child has this goal as its basis and has undoubtedly resulted in the creation of more than a few stars.

Ours, however, is an age of specialization and keen competition and it is naive to assume that this sort of childbearing technique is confined to the world of show business. Below are some examples:

The Architecture Mother

The architecture mother does indeed have her work cut out for her. Her days are filled with the difficult task of impressing upon her youngster the need for economy of line and the desirability of wiping one's feet before coming into the machine for living. Other mothers have children who pay attention, who realize that form should follow function, and that there's such a thing as considering the reflective qualities of glass *before* going out to play. Other mothers can relax once in a while because their children listen the *first* time without having to be told over and over again, until I'm sick of hearing myself say it, *"Less, less, I mean it, less.* And I'm *not* going to say it again."

The Television Talk Show Host Mother

Here is a job that presents such a multiplicity of problems that relatively few have entered the field. The work is arduous and the hours long, for it is still too soon to tell whether the child will be early morning, mid-afternoon, or late night. Hardly a facet of modern life can be disregarded. "Vegas, darling, the 'Las' is strictly for *them*. Just plain Vegas. That's right. Now what do we do in Vegas? No, darling, that's what *they* do in Vegas. *We play* Vegas. We *are playing* Vegas. We *played* Vegas. Let's not forget our grammar. Let's have a little consideration for the English language here, please. Now, when we play Vegas what else do we do? That's right—*kill them. Kill them* in Vegas. *Killing them* in Vegas. *Killed them* in Vegas. And what do we do when things get interesting? Well, yes, we can bleep sometimes, but that's not what pays allowances, is it? That's not what buys bicycles. No. We sell a little something. We cut to a commercial. We have a word from our sponsors and we break the stations. Good. Now, here's a book. What do we do with books? No, and I don't want to have to say it again, *we* don't read books. You want to read books or you want to be a

television talk show host? You can't have it both
ways. We don't *read* books. We *mean* to read books.
And where do we mean to read books? That's
right—*on the plane. We meant to read it on the plane.*
And why didn't we? Come on, we've been
through this a thousand times. I'll give you a
hint—but this is the last time. O.K., here's the
hint—it starts with *D*. That's right, Duke. We
meant to read it on the plane but we ran into the
Duke—Duke Wayne. Very good, darling, terrif-
fic. I think that's enough for tonight. Just a
minute, young man, where do you think *you're*
going? To bed? Really? Without a quick rundown
of tomorrow night's guests? That's how you
leave a room? Very nice. Excellent. Eighteen
hours a day with this and you just leave the room
without a quick rundown of tomorrow night's
guests. That's no way to be a television talk
show host and if you don't learn now you're
going to find out later the hard way. *I mean it.* I
don't like to say it—I *am* your mother—but you're
going to be canceled, I mean it. What? Who?
Cloris Leachman? Gore Vidal? Shecky Green?
Dr. Joyce Brothers and Jim Bouton? That's my
baby. You're a beautiful guy, darling. Good
night."

The Mortician Mother

The burden borne by the mortician mother is
not an easy one. For she must spend virtually
every waking hour policing the behavior of her

child. Is that *giggling* she hears? Wearily she must go to his room and admonish him for the ten thousandth time, "Could you look a little somber, please? I mean, is that too much to ask? A little dignity? A little sorrowful understanding? Other kids manage to look somber without having to be told every twenty seconds. Other kids can be trusted alone for ten minutes without a lot of laughter. Other kids don't shrug their shoulders and walk away when their mothers ask for a little opinion on how they look—other kids say, 'Very lifelike' in a nice hushed tone the first time they're asked. Other kids can wear a carnation a whole day without it wilting. I don't know where I went wrong with you. I don't know where you got this taste for simplicity, not even simplicity; just ordinary cheapness if you ask me. Oh yes, don't think I don't know about that plain pine box you've got in here. I'm not stupid. Well, let me tell you something, Mr. Know-It-All. There is such a thing as solid mahogany with real brass fittings and satin lining and the sooner you learn that the better off you'll be."

The Headwaiter Mother

Few appreciate the problems that beset the mother of the aspiring headwaiter. Not only has she to contend with the difficulty of instilling in him a passion for the unnecessary flourish but she must also curb his every naïve instinct for friendliness. "How many times have I told you not to answer the first time you're spoken to? *How many?* And what is this *helpful business* all of a sudden, may I ask? Where did you pick *that* up? Is *that* what you want to be when you grow up? *Helpful?* Fine. Wonderful. Go, be helpful. Be a Boy Scout for all I care. Yes, a Boy Scout—because that's how you'll end up if you don't stop fooling around. *I'm* not the one who wants to be a headwaiter. I'm not the one who said, 'Oh, Mommy, if you mold me into a headwaiter I'll never ask you for another thing, not ever.' So I'm not the one who'll suffer. You want to be a headwaiter? *Act* like a headwaiter. A little ignoring, please. A little uncalled-for arrogance. You want to be obsequious? Believe me, there's a time and a place. Princess Grace comes in, David Rockefeller, Tennessee Williams, O.K., fine, good, *then* be obsequious—you have my blessing. But I don't want to see it all the time. I don't want to see it for some expense account jerk who's out on the town. I don't want to see it for every leisure suit with two on the aisle for *A Chorus Line.* Understand? A little more influence peddling and a little less with the warm welcome, O.K.? Your father and I aren't going to be here forever, you know."

The Restaurant Critic Mother

The restaurant critic mother is a proud woman. So proud, in fact, that those who know her have pretty much had it up to here with listening to what a picky eater she's got on her hands. But her pride is understandable, for she has earned it. For years she has asked, "How was lunch, dear?" only to be answered with a terse "O.K." Over and over again she has drilled her little charge until the happy day when her question elicits this rewarding response: "Mommy, the sandwich was superb. The Wonder Bread softly unobtrusive, the perfect foil for both the richly poignant Superchunky Skippy and the clear, fragrant Welch's grape. The carrot sticks were exquisitely sweet, yet asserted their integrity in every glorious crunch. The Yoo Hoo was interesting—adolescent but robust—and the Yankee Doodle, a symphony of snowy creme filling and rich, dark cake; the whole of it bathed in a splendor of chocolate-flavored icing that verged on the sinful."

Specialty Banking:
A Numbered Account

Not so long ago, in Manhattan's fashionable East Fifties, there appeared an institution called the First Women's Bank. This prompted me to speculate:

1. Is this a mere fad or an actual trend?
2. What is the First Women's Bank really like?
3. Can we look forward to the opening of a competitive establishment to be known as the Other Women's Bank?

I have mulled this over and have been successful in formulating answers to all three questions. My original intention was to answer these questions in order, but I eventually chose another plan of action. Lest you get the wrong impression, I hasten to assure that this in no way constitutes a flamboyant display of perversity. It is simply that I changed my mind—which is, after all, a woman's prerogative.

What Is the First Women's Bank Really Like?

Rather than attempt to answer this question by utilizing the methods of the investigative reporter—legwork, research, and digging for facts—I decided instead to employ those of the irresponsible wag: lying on the sofa, talking on the phone, and making things up. This procedure proved quite satisfactory and has resulted in the following report.

The First Women's Bank is called the First Women's Bank only in deference to convention. It is not the real name. The real name is Separate Checks. When a typical customer (for the purposes of clarity we'll call her Jane Doe) enters the bank she has three windows from which to choose:

1. PAYING: BACK
2. IS: RECEIVING
3. NO: ACCOUNTING: FOR TASTE

Should Jane find these departments inadequate for her needs and experience a momentary loss of faith, she has only to remember that her bank offers every possible convenience—a Christmas Club, a Hanukkah Club, and a Bridge Club—in order to regain her former confidence. Thus fortified, even the knowledge that the bank closes two or three days a month for cramps will not deter her from venturing into the area reserved for a more serious business. Here she will be confronted by a neat row of desks, each sporting a dignified oblong nameplate: Madge, Delores, Wilma, and Mary Beth respectively. Jane chooses Mary Beth and sits down. Mary Beth pours Jane a cup of coffee, apologizes for the state of her blotter, and asks Jane what's bothering her. When Jane asks Mary Beth how she knew something was bothering her, Mary Beth just smiles and says, "Woman's intuition." Jane explains to Mary Beth that she needs to borrow eleven hundred dollars to repair her car, which was severely damaged in an accident resulting from Jane's attempt to execute a sharp right turn while applying lip gloss. Jane is eager to have the car fixed before her husband returns from his business trip. Mary Beth understands, of course, and an arrangement is made whereby Separate Checks agrees to lend Jane eleven hundred dollars if Jane will lend Separate Checks eight place settings of her good silver for their next board luncheon. Her business successfully concluded, Jane takes her leave—happily reciting the bank's catchy slogan, "Bottom Dollar: Tops to Match." She is eleven hundred dollars richer and more firmly convinced than ever that Separate Checks is the permanent wave of the future.

Is This a Mere Fad or an Actual Trend?

The answer to this question is "An actual trend." The success of Separate Checks will cause an outbreak of specialty banks, each catering to an extremely specific group.

Children

This institution will be called the First National Piggy Bank. It will offer to its customers a unique service—Banking by Color. It will be fully equipped with high-quality crayons, which will be attached to anchored chains. The bank's motto will be "Our Checks Bounce Higher Than Yours Do," and instead of patterns, its checks will be available in a variety of flavors: Red Raspberry, Chocolate Marshmallow, Vanilla Fudge, and Black Cherry. The employees will be kind but firm, and those dealing with the more intricate procedures such as Advance on Next Week's Allowance Loans will sit behind desks bearing their nameplates—Uncle Ralph, Aunt Marcia, Uncle Harold, and Auntie Ruthie. Should one of the customers default on such a loan he will be sent to his room without dessert for 6½ percent of each month he is overdue. If this fails to bring about the desired result the bank will have no recourse but to garnishee the debtor's birthday money until the loan is repaid. Hours: After School and On the Weekend When the Homework Is Finished.

Homosexuals

The First National Raving Bank will distinguish itself by being the only bank in town with a two-drink minimum. Special features include the availability of three-dollar bills and checks bearing either a portrait of Ronald Firbank or all of the lyrics to "Somewhere over the Rainbow." Should a customer of the bank wish to apply for a credit card he need only enter the business area, where he will find Mr. Eugene, Mr. Randy, and

Mr. Joel, and Eduardo, ready and willing to furnish him with the information that Master Charge isn't the only game in town. Hours: After.

Psychiatrists

The New York Bank of Self-Pity will not be housed in a single building but rather in a complex, since nothing is that simple. If one of the customers is overdrawn he can attempt to convince the bank to make good his check, as it was their inability to deal realistically with figures that caused the error. If he is desirous of establishing a more meaningful relationship with his account he is free to lie down and discuss it with one of the self-destructive and immature employees. The pens in this bank are thoughtfully equipped with ink that blots symbolically. Hours: 10:10–10:50.

Can We Look Forward to the Opening of a Competitive Establishment to Be Known as the Other Women's Bank?

Undoubtedly. The telltale signs will be safety deposit boxes filled with expensive baubles, a sultry look, and a tendency to be alone at Christmas. Hours. Tuesday and Thursday Afternoons.

The Right of Eminent Domain Versus the Rightful Dominion of the Eminent

Generally speaking, laws are designed to protect the public from harm. Generally speaking, harm is seen as physical peril. Generally speaking, physical peril is not a particularly interesting subject. True, there are those laws which endeavor to shield the public from financial disaster. Truer still, financial disaster occurs anyway. And truest of all, the public is not a particularly interesting group.

Thus our system of law is something less than captivating, for it consistently fails to deal with the three questions of greatest concern. The three questions of greatest concern are:

1. Is it attractive?
2. Is it amusing?
3. Does it know its place?

One can see at a glance that these three questions not only encompass all contingencies covered by the present system but, more importantly, they confront without flinching the genuine hazards of modern life. They are therefore the only possible basis for any reasonable system of justice. And henceforth they shall be regarded as such. If you must reply in the negative to any of these questions you are committing an illegal act. For the purposes of clarity I shall consider each question separately, although it should be quite apparent that they are all three as brothers.

Is It Attractive?

When I was in grammar school it was customary at the beginning of each year for the teacher to explain the principle of individual freedom in a democracy by stating: "Your right to swing your arm ends where the other person's nose begins." An admirable sentiment—unquestionably. But one somehow lacking in that little something extra that makes it all worthwhile.

Quite simply, it misses the point. I, for one, would much rather be punched in the nose than in the sensibility. And so I offer this in its stead: "Your right to wear a mint-green polyester leisure suit ends where it meets my eye." Should you choose to disregard this dictate you shall be arrested for bad taste.

In order to administer to all of the worms that will come crawling out of this hitherto unopened can there will be appointed a Commissar of Good Looks who shall issue a manifesto detailing the following offenses:

    A. The Construction of Buildings That Look Like Gigantic Electric Shavers.

B. Television Commercials and Magazine Advertisements That Use Real People Instead of Models.

C. Cigarettes That Come in a Choice of Colors: If White Ones Were Good Enough for Edward R. Murrow They're Good Enough for You.

D. Ice Cubes That Come in a Choice of Shapes: Flowers Belong in One's Lapel, Not in One's Bourbon.

E. Airports That Have Fallen into the Hands of Graphic Designers with a Penchant for Bold Simplicity.

F. Furniture Made to Resemble Objects That Were Played with by Small Children in the Nineteen-Forties.

G. Long-sleeved T-Shirts Stenciled to Look Like Dinner Jackets and Invariably Worn by Those Who Would Have Occasion to Wear a Dinner Jacket Only While at Work.

The penalty for those responsible for any of the above-mentioned crimes shall be ninety days spent in the company of the inventor of the male centerfold or seventy-two months in Los Angeles—whichever comes first.

Is It Amusing?

Once upon a time, long, long ago, people wanted to be well spoken. Those capable of an elegant turn of phrase were much admired. Wit was in great demand. It was the day of the epigram.

Time went on, and by and by it came to pass

that people were chiefly interested in being well liked. Those capable of a firm handshake were much admired. Friendliness was in great demand. It was the day of the telegram.

Presently it appears that people are mainly concerned with being well rested. Those capable of uninterrupted sleep are much admired. Unconsciousness is in great demand. This is the day of the milligram.

Far be it from me to make noise while you're asleep but I should like to notify you that you are under arrest for being boring. The Commissar of a Way with Words suspects you of one or more of the following:

> A. Rather Than Attempt the Art of Conversation You Prefer to Communicate with Your Fellow Man by Hugging Strangers Who Are Reliving the Bad Parts of Their Childhood While Immersed in a Swimming Pool Filled with Warm Water.
>
> B. You Think That the Women's Liberation Movement *Does* Have a Sense of Humor.
>
> C. You Use in Conversation Phrases That Appear on T-Shirts.
>
> D. You Share David Susskind's Apparently Inexhaustible Interest in the Private Lives of Deservedly Unknown Homosexuals.
>
> E. You Feel the Need to Discuss Your Innermost Thoughts on a Weekly Basis with Six Other People, One of Whom Is Being Paid to Listen.
>
> F. You No Longer Feel the Need to Discuss Your Innermost Thoughts on a Weekly Basis with Six Other People, One of Whom Is Being Paid to Listen, Because You Feel That

Erica Jong Has Said It All for You.

G. The Letters est Have Meaning for You Beyond Eastern Standard Time.

H. You Are the Host of a Television Talk Show Who So Firmly Believes That Everyone in the Whole World Is Just About to Play Las Vegas for Two Weeks That You Introduce Your Next Guest as "Dr. Jonas Salk—a Beautiful Guy."

Should you be found guilty you shall be sentenced to a one-year subscription to *Psychology Today* or seventy-two months in Los Angeles—whichever comes first.

Does It Know Its Place?

Under the jurisdiction of the Commissar of What Is Appropriate the adage "A place for everything and everything in its place" has been broadened to include "A place for everyone and everyone in their place." You are not in your place or are responsible for something not being in *its* place if you are to blame in any of these instances:

A. You Are a Man Who Attends Consciousness-raising Meetings.

B. You Are a Woman Who Attends Consciousness-raising Meetings.

C. You Are a Dog and You Live in New York, Probably in My Neighborhood.

D. You Are an Army Camouflage Combat Uniform Being Worn by Someone Who Is Not a Soldier in Southeast Asia.

E. You Are Wall-to-Wall Carpeting and You
    Are in the Bathroom.
F. You Are on Your Way over to My Apartment
    and You Have Not Called First.
G. You Write Poetry and You Are Not Dead.

Those convicted of any of the above-
mentioned crimes shall be subject to being either
a dessert served in a brandy snifter or seventy-
two months in Los Angeles—whichever comes
first.

The Family Affair:
A Moral Tale

The addition of the prefix *natural* to the word *childbirth* assumed that there was such a thing as unnatural childbirth. Advocates of this concept pointed out that for thousands of years people had babies in the privacy and quietude of their own homes or rice paddies simply by lying down and breathing deeply. This business of rushing to the hospital, being shot up with drugs, and attended by doctors was wrong. It was not meant to be. Some listened. Some did not. Some of those who did not, did not arrogantly, with a strong, pure belief in the righteousness of their unnaturalness. They liked rushing to the hospital. They loved being shot up with drugs. They adored being attended to by doctors. To them unnaturalness was the way of life. Secure in their commitment to artificiality, they greeted each other with knowing looks and bade each other good-bye with a whispered " à rebours." They were content and they believed themselves to be as sophisticated as was possible under the circumstances, which were undeniably heterosexual and therefore limited.

Then little by little there began to circulate among this group an unsettling rumor. Dark mutterings were heard. The fast crowd was seen less and less frequently in the better waiting rooms. After months of hushed speculation the truth was uncovered: a certain chichi element had found a way to have children that made mere unnatural childbirth look like eating your own placenta. This set had entirely dispensed with bodily function and were obtaining their children in bars.

The most popular of these bars was called Chicken Little and was located in a brownstone on a fashionable street near the East River. Prospective parents on the prowl would arrive at this establishment by taxi or private car, knock smartly on the lacquered chocolate-brown door, and present themselves to a deceptively kind-looking septuagenarian known only as the Grandmother.

Upon passing muster, they either sat at small tables or leaned against the bar and tried to look loving as they cruised the children. They talked very little and then only to remark on the quality of the trade with such comments as "Think he looks like me?" "There's a student council president if I ever saw one," and "Do you think she'll make her bed?" The most aggressive were known to sidle right up to promising-looking tots and murmur, "Like to play catch, fella?" Or to take particularly blond little girls aside, slip them homemade chocolate chip cookies, and let them know in no uncertain terms that there were plenty more where those came from.

The children were not without ploys of their

own and some of the little tykes would stop at nothing. As the evening wore on and most of the really permissive-looking adults had been picked off, it was not uncommon for the desperate unadopted to be seen furtively applying calculatingly cute arrays of freckles across the bridges of their little noses with cleverly concealed brown eyebrow pencils, or announcing in loud, bound-to-be-overheard voices that when they grew up they wanted to be doctors.

No careful observer of this scene could help but notice that certain patrons bypassed the main area and headed immediately for the back room. The back room was reserved for those with more specialized tastes. Here the toddlers would leave one of their overall suspenders unbuttoned to indicate their special preference. An unbuttoned left suspender meant: I talk back. . . . I don't do my homework. . . . I will wet my bed until I am fifteen. . . . I will make your life a living hell. . . . You won't know what you did to deserve me. This group quickly gravitated toward the adults who carried their cigarettes in their right hands, which meant: Don't worry, we'll work it out. . . . How can I help? . . . I didn't mean it that way. . . . Where did I go wrong?

An unbuttoned right suspender meant: It was my fault. . . . I'll try to do better. . . . I cannot tell a lie. . . . I guess I'm just no good. This gang invariably found their way to the adults carrying their cigarettes in their left hands, which meant: No dessert. . . . Go to your room. . . . I threw them away. . . . *We* don't have Christmas.

As you can well imagine, a situation such as this could not go on forever. Other unnaturally inclined parents began to flock to Chicken Little. Soon they were coming in from out of town. "The weekends," said the cognoscenti, "are absolutely impossible. I mean, did you see those children in there last week? Strictly Remedial Reading, I mean really."

Finally all this activity attracted the attention of the police and late one Saturday night Chicken Little was raided. "Up against the wall, mother luckers!" shouted the cops to a group of children holding tightly to the hands of suspiciously aproned women. "Hell no, we won't grow!" the children screamed back. Suddenly a little boy broke loose from his newly acquired mother, ran to the bar, and grabbed for a bottle of milk. "Hold it right there!" yelled the officers of the law. Their warning went unheeded and the little boy was quickly joined by three other children of the sort who don't know when to stop. They all drank greedily from their respective bottles and fixed the police with impish grins, flaunting their milk mustaches. The boys in blue, pushed beyond their limits, let loose with a volley of fire. All four children were killed. And such was the tragedy of Quenched State.

Guide and Seek:
I'm OK, You're Not

Throughout history, people have exhibited an unfortunate tendency to band together in groups. The reasons for this phenomenon vary widely but they *can* be divided into two general categories: common need and common desire. In the common need division (and I assure you that the word *common* has not been carelessly chosen) we find such things as leftish political parties, barn raisings, prides of lions, gay liberation, retirement communities, *Ms.* magazine, armies, quilting bees, the Rockettes, and est-type programs.

Under the heading of common desire— previous parenthetical comment likewise applicable—belong rightish political parties, exercise classes, the Chicago Seven, entourages, the New School for Social Research, fun crowds, and est-type programs. That some, if not all, of the particulars in each category seem to be interchangeable is due to the fact that need and desire are, like cotton madras, inclined to bleed.

The more vigilant among you may have observed that est-type programs appear in both categories. The reason for this is twofold: one, because those who participate in such programs are as desirous as they are needful, and two, because such programs are the very essence of groupness and therefore the most spectacularly unattractive. That I am totally devoid of sympathy for, or interest in, the world of groups is directly attributable to the fact that *my* two greatest needs and desires—smoking cigarettes and plotting revenge—are basically solitary pursuits. Oh, sure, sometimes a friend or two drops by and we light up together and occasionally I bounce a few vengeance ideas around with a willing companion, but actual meetings are really unnecessary.

I am therefore dismayed that programs such as est seem to be proliferating at a rate of speed traditionally associated with the more unpleasant amoebic disorders—rate of speed being only one of their shared characteristics. As this craze for personal fulfillment shows no signs of abatement, I am afraid that we shall soon be witness to programs catering to needs and desires hitherto considered overly specific. Following are a few possibilities.

rip

rip, an acronym for *rest in pleasure*, is an organization for those deceased who feel for one reason or another that they are just not getting enough out of death. The name of the leader of this group is not known—he is, at best, an elusive figure but it is generally accepted that *rip* was started in response to the needs of a small coterie who often confided in one another their sporadic fears that somehow they really didn't feel *that* dead. Thus it is believed that Judge Crater, God, Amelia Earhart, Adolf Hitler, and the Lindbergh Baby are responsible for the foundation of this program.

The insecurely departed meet whenever the spirit moves them and their sessions consist largely of answering honestly a series of settling questions on the order of: "Are you saving your receipts?" "Are you coughing?" "Are you on a low-carbohydrate diet?" "Are you waiting for a check?" "Are you on hold?" "No?" responds the leader. "Then obviously you are dead. If you are dead there is no way you are not having eternal peace. If you are having eternal peace you are free from responsibility and the eventuality of being annoyed. There you have it. What could be more pleasant?"

There are certain deprivations attendant to *rip* sessions. Members are not allowed to go to the bathroom, to stretch their legs, or to eat. And although there have been no complaints from members, there are always those skeptics, those malcontents, those tearer-downers, who are convinced that were *rip* properly investigated more than one skeleton would come tumbling out of the closet.

lack

lack, or *l* outish *a* nd *c* rass *k* ollective is a program dedicated to the proposition that vulgarity and bad taste are an inalienable right. The *lackies*, as they are sometimes called, meet if they feel like it at program headquarters, which is known as La Gaucherie. La Gaucherie is densely furnished with seven thousand always-in-operation console color televisions, nine hundred constantly blaring quadrophonic stereos, shag rugs in six hundred and seventy-eight decorator colors, and an eclectic mix of Mediterranean-style dining room sets, fun sofas, interesting wall hangings, and modular seating systems. These members not otherwise occupied practicing the electric guitar or writing articles for *Playgirl* sit around in unduly comfortable positions expressing their honest feelings and opinions in loud tones of voice. Male *lackies* are encouraged to leave unbuttoned the first five buttons of their shirts unless they have unusually pale skin and hairy chests, in which case they are *required* to do so. Female members are encouraged to encourage them. Both sexes participate in a form of meditation that consists of breathing deeply of musk oil while wearing synthetic fabrics. The eventual goal of this discipline is to reach the state of mind known as Los Angeles.

hurts'

hurts stands for *h*ypochondriacs *u*sually *r* terribly *sick*, and sessions, which are called clinics, are held every twenty minutes in a hall known as the Waiting Room. The members file in, sit on uncomfortable leather-look couches, and read old issues of *Today's Health* until the leader, a tall, distinguished, graying-at-the-temples gentleman named Major Medical, calls the meeting to order. Members must undergo an initiation ritual, the Blood Test, before they can compare symptoms. Symptom comparison varies from session to session but all who belong to *hurts* are ever mindful of the program's motto, "There's no such thing as *just* a mole." Not infrequently the symptom comparison gets out of hand as each victim tries to outdo the other. On such occasions Major Medical finds it necessary to remind the group members of the sacred oath they took when they received the privilege of wearing the Blue Cross, and must admonish them with a painfully intoned "Patients, patients."

A World View

Departure

I board a Trans World Airlines jet to Milan the first stop on my whirlwind tour of the Continent. The plane is full of Italians (something I hadn't quite counted on). I am armed with three cartons of duty-free Vantage cigarettes and a long list of phone numbers I know I will never use. I mean I just can't see myself calling someone and saying, "Hello, you don't know me but my hair dresser occasionally sleeps with your press agent, so why don't you show me Paris." The flight is uneventful except that the gentleman to my left, a Milanese flour manufacturer wearing a green mohair suit, falls in love with me and I am compelled to spend the last three hours of the trip pretending to be in a coma.

Milan

Milan is quite an attractive little city. A nice cathedral, *The Last Supper*, a very glamorous train station built by Mussolini, la Scala, and many other enjoyable sights. There are two kinds of people in Milan. The people who work for the various *Vogues* and the people who don't. The people who work for the various *Vogues* are very sociable and enjoy going out. The people who don't work for the various *Vogues* may also be very sociable but they probably don't speak much English. Almost everybody I meet in Milan is a Communist, particularly the rich. Milan is a very political place and the city is full of Communist graffiti and soldiers. Everyone in Milan is very well dressed.

In Milan you do not get matches for free. A double book of matches costs one hundred lire, which is more than fifteen cents in real money. I was appalled by this and resented it tremendously whenever anyone asked me for a light. Whenever anyone *offered* me a light I was overwhelmed by this largesse and felt that I had won something.

There is a severe change shortage in Italy. When you make a purchase that requires that the shopkeeper give you back coins he gives you candies or stamps instead. If this should happen to you, you should under no circumstances handle these stamps cavalierly. There are apparently no post offices in Italy, so if you want stamps this is your best bet. Everyone in Milan works and if it rains in Milan they blame it on Rome.

Rome

Nobody in Rome works and if it rains in Rome *and* they happen to notice it they blame it on Milan. In Rome people spend most of their time having lunch. And they do it very well—Rome is unquestionably the lunch capital of the world. Rome is very architectural and they have quite a lot of art there. The Romans are very nice people and interested in the opinions of others. As you leave the Vatican Museums you will notice to your right a suggestion box. I suggested that they put an acoustical tile ceiling in the Sistine Chapel to cut down on the incredible din produced by the German tourists. They could then reproduce all of Michelangelo's scenes in acrylic paint, thereby preserving the form *and* adding a little function.

I was in Rome for about two weeks, during which time there were five major strikes. I don't know what the strikers wanted or whether or not they got it, but it probably didn't matter. Going on strike in Rome is much more a matter of style than it is of economics. Rome is a very loony city in every respect. One needs but spend an hour or two there to realize that Fellini makes documentaries.

There is no such thing as rock and roll in Italy, so all the kids there want to be movie stars instead of heroin addicts. This is very pertinent news if you have a taste for the underaged because it means that it is possible to have an entire conversation with a fifteen-year-old without feeling as if you have to throw up.

Cannes: The Film Festival

Cannes is very cute. Lots of big white hotels, pretty beaches, starlets, yachts, lavish parties, a casino, and people who speak English. Everybody in Cannes is very busy. The producers are busy trying to get things to produce. The directors are busy trying to get things to direct. The buyers are busy trying to get sellers. The sellers are busy trying to get buyers. And the waiters are busy trying not to take your order. The best way to meet people in Cannes is to sit on the Carleton Terrace and order a drink. A few hours later the waiter will bring you somebody else's martini. You pick up the martini in an extravagant manner and look around. A few tables away someone will be holding your Perrier with a twist in a quizzical position and you will be well on your way to making a friend and/or deal.

There are about two hundred films a day shown in Cannes. I saw two and a half. It costs a lot of money to get to France and I can go to the movies in New York. Anyway, you know what they say about screening rooms—in the dark they all look alike.

Paris

Paris is a great beauty. As such it possesses all the qualities that one finds in any other great beauty: chic, sexiness, grandeur, arrogance, and the absolute inability and refusal to listen to reason. So if you're going there you would do well to remember this: no matter how politely or distinctly you ask a Parisian a question he will persist in answering you in French.

Notes on "Trick"

> trick, *n.* from OFr. *trichier*, to trick, to cheat; Pr. *tric*, deceit; *It. treccare*, to cheat. 1. an action or device designed to deceive, swindle, etc.; artifice; a dodge; ruse; stratagem; deception. 2. a practical joke; a mischievous or playful act; prank.... 4. (a) a clever or difficult act intended to amuse...(b) any feat requiring skill. 5. the art, method, or process of doing something successfully or of getting a result quickly... 6. an expedient or convention of an art, craft, or trade... 7. a personal mannerism...

I have chosen these definitions, carefully selected from the Unabridged Second Edition of Webster's Dictionary, on the basis of congeniality with what is perhaps the most current usage of the word *Trick* —that which refers to the object of one's affectations. By "one" I mean the person of serious ambition in those fields most likely to necessitate the employment of a press agent. Such a person is often, but not always, a homosexual; the primary reason for this being that the heterosexual is far too burdened by his own young to be much interested in anyone else's. Where the heterosexual feels a sense of duty, a sense of honor, a sense of responsibility,

the homosexual feels a sense of humor, a sense of
protocol, and most significantly, a sense of
design.

With no dependents, he is free to pursue his
selfish interests—among these, the Trick. The
Trick allows one a semblance of romantic
intimacy without the risk that one's own
importance will be improperly appreciated.

The Trick exhibits those qualities found in a
favorite toy. Surely, no sane person would if he
could help it knowingly choose a doll that talked
about progressive education and demanded that
one share the housework—and it is precisely this
ability to help it that separates the men from the
toys.

Fortunately, there are many available to fill the
role of Trick, since the first requirement of the
climber is a toehold. In allowing this close
proximity one is, indeed, apt to have one's pocket
picked, but one also has the option of causing a
nasty spill. It is, therefore, a situation in which
everyone concerned can be taken advantage of to
the best of his ability. As to the question of who
runs the greatest risk of getting hurt, one can
only reply that the number of mountains that
have suffered severe or fatal injury is infinitesi-
mal when compared to the number who have
tackled them.

The word Trick is used to describe the less
illustrious member of such an alliance and it fills a
genuine need. For the noteworthy partner the
words Rich and/or Famous are quite sufficient,
but the corresponding adjectives of Cute and/or

Well-built are somewhat lacking. Actual names were all right for home use, but neither "Juan" nor "Heather" is really serviceable as a generic term.

Exactly when or why the word Trick was first used for this purpose is unclear, although there is a theory that it derives from the slang of prostitutes, who have long used it in regard to their clients. While this contention is not without logic it is far more likely that this use of the word Trick was spread by simple (or complex) word of mouth.

I have in the interest of clarification jotted down some notes on the subject, but before we proceed to them there are a few things that must be said:

> Tricks like to lie in bed—also in restaurants.
>
> *   *   *
>
> Tricks should never be left strewn carelessly about the house where someone might trip over them.
>
> *   *   *
>
> Tricks are attracted to bright objects. This may elude your understanding since you obviously do not share this tendency.

These notes are for Lord Alfred Douglas.

1. It is wise to avoid the very young Trick. For while it is indeed true that they offer the advantage of having to leave early to get to school, it is equally true that the very same thing

can be accomplished by the use of fashion models, who will not only have to be standing on top of the Pan Am Building in full makeup by 8 A.M. but who also will never need help with their term papers on John Donne.

2. The homosexual's desire to remain youthful is entirely based on his knowledge that he will never have children and hence will be deprived of legitimately meeting their more attractive friends.

3. There are those for whom the most highly prized quality in a Trick is sheer stupidity. Of this group the most envied is an eminent film director who has installed in his residence a young man whose lips move when he watches television.

4. Random examples of items that are part of the canon of Trick:

Bennington College's Nonresident Term
Conceptual art
Stealing
Trying on someone else's leather jacket while he's at work
Artistic greeting cards
Interesting food
Black sheets
Remembering telephone numbers by making a word out of the corresponding letters
Trying to figure things out by listening to the lyrics of popular songs
Exotic cigarettes
Reading, or more likely watching, *Breakfast at Tiffany's* and identifying with Holly Golightly
Hearing about F. Scott Fitzgerald and thinking you're Zelda

Being Zelda Fitzgerald and thinking you're F.
  Scott
Lina Wertmuller movies seen without nausea
Stag movies seen with lust

5. A good Trick, like a good child, is mannerly.
He does not speak unless spoken to, he does not
contradict, and he kneels when an adult comes
into the room.

> "Still as interested as ever in the young, I see,"
> Francis remarked in a confidential undertone,
> glancing round the obstruction of his friend's
> shoulders to where Daniel stood....."You old
> succubus! Let's have a look at your latest suffix!"
>
> —*The Apes of God,*
>   Wyndham Lewis

6. Mixed company in the modern sense of the
term means that Tricks are present. How often
one has longed to be left alone after dinner while
the Tricks go upstairs and take cocaine.

7. American industry has made a grave error
in overlooking the Trick. The market is wide
open and would be rewardingly receptive to such
products as strawberry-swirl vodka, Hermes
mittens, and a pack of cigarettes with a secret
surprise inside.

8. Although the male Trick is more prone to
stealing than is the female, neither sex can be
trusted alone in the same room with an invitation
to a party at Halston's.

9. Tricks have feelings too, as they will be the
first to tell you. If you prick them they do indeed

bleed—usually your good vodka.

10. The Trick is, when it comes to finance, truly a child of the modern age, for he never carries cash—at least not his own.

11. Other people's Tricks pose a special problem. Upon coming across a friend thus accompanied you must, out of politeness, treat the Trick amicably. This is invariably a mistake, for shortly thereafter the friend will divest himself of his consort and for the rest of your life the Trick will be coming up to you at parties and saying hello.

12. The simple black Trick is always appropriate—particularly at events where food is not served.

13. It is not unusual for the male aficionado to draw his Tricks exclusively from the lower orders. Such a person is, indeed, often attracted to the criminal element. When asked wherein lay the appeal, a spokesman for this group replied, "Everybody looks good when they're under arrest."

> "Horace has always been like that—his intentions have *always* been strictly honourable" sneered Ratner "and he has never lost his belief in 'genius'—associated *always* with extreme youth, and a pretty face! Unfortunately, the type of beauty which appeals to Horace you see is rather commonplace. The result is Horace has never actually met with a 'genius,' which is a pity. It might have opened his eyes if he had!"
>
> —*The Apes of God*,
> Wyndham Lewis

14. Should you be awakened in the middle of the night by a faint scratching sound, do not fear for your health unless you are certain that all valuables have been safely locked away. For it is far less likely that your Trick is suffering a communicable rash than that he is copying out your address book. The more vindictive among you may be interested in devising a phony version of said book in which you have carefully set down the phone numbers of particularly vile ex-Tricks next to the names of your most prestigious and least favorite former employers.

15. The mistreatment of Tricks is the revenge of the intelligent upon the beautiful.

16. Regrettably few Tricks are attractive enough to be allowed to discuss their innermost thoughts. Only those possessed of truly incredible cheekbones should ever be permitted to use the word *energy* in a sentence unless they are referring to heating oil.

17. The Trick is not an equal but he is often an equalizer.

18. Occasionally a Trick will succeed so spectacularly that he will make the transition to person. When this occurs he will assume a truly amazing imperiousness of manner. People love to feel superior to their past.

19. Tricks almost always have pets. This is understandable, as everyone needs someone they can talk to on their own level.

20. Taking an emergency telephone call from a Dr. Juan or a Dr. Heather is certain to result in overinvolvement.

21. There is a distinct Trick taste in literature.

Among favorite Trick books are those dealing
with the quest for God, such as the works of
Carlos Castaneda and Hermann Hesse; those
depicting a glamorous and torturous homosexu-
ality, as in the case of *Nightwood* by Djuna Barnes;
and those assuring Tricks that everything is fine
and dandy, especially them. This sort of reading
is generally harmless providing they have
mastered the technique of reading quietly to
themselves. For even the most hopelessly
smitten will bridle at being awakened by Anaïs
Nin.

22. When it comes to the visual arts a marked
Trick preference is also evident. Work that falls
into this category is easy to recognize, as the
Trick is unfailingly attracted to that which looks
as if he could (or did) make it himself.

23. Art movies on television are ideal for
luring the reluctant Trick to one's apartment.
There are very few people who dabble in this field
who have not seen the first twenty minutes of
Loves of a Blonde more times than they care to
count.

24. The Trick is, without fail, drawn to the
interesting job. Interesting jobs, in this sense,
include not only work in museum gift shops but
also minor positions on the production crews of
documentary films concerning birth defects.

25. The Trick, more often than not, will
display an unconquerable bent for creativity. The
East Coast Trick leans heavily toward the
composition of free-verse poetry, while his West
Coast counterpart goes in for songwriting.

Tricks of all regions own expensive cameras with which they take swaggeringly grainy photographs of nearby planets and sensitive young drug addicts. This is not difficult to understand, as they are relentless admirers of that which they call art and you call hobbies.

> "Can't you see Dan that you are Horace's plaything—When he talks about your 'genius'—pulling your leg—that's to get your 'genius'!—*People always pull other people's legs when they want to get hold of their genius!"*

> —*The Apes of God*,
> Wyndham Lewis

26. One man's Trick is another man's design assistant.

27. A New York hostess with a penchant for young boys gave a dinner at which a kind and fatherly magazine editor found himself seated across from her Trick. Seeking to put the boy at ease, the editor asked him politely what he did. "I'm an alchemist," the boy replied. Overhearing the exchange, another guest whispered, "Alchemist? They *used* to be bank clerks."

28. There is occasionally some question as to which member of a given duo *is* the Trick. This sort of confusion results when one (the elder) has money and the other (the younger) has talent. In such cases, and with all due respect to rising young luminaries, unless the money is exceedingly new and the talent exceedingly large, the money, as is its wont, wins. Or as was once said to

a somewhat braggardly young artist while window-shopping at Porthaults, "If she has *those* sheets, you're the Trick."

29. Tricks like you for what they aren't. You like Tricks for what you haven't.

30. If one half of the couple is a waiter or waitress, he or she is always the Trick. Particularly, or in the case of New York City inevitably, if he or she has artistic ambitions. Such individuals may indeed traffic with those that they in turn refer to as Tricks, but that is a level of society far too submerged to be of any interest.

31. At public gatherings Tricks have been observed speaking to one another. What they actually say can only be a matter of conjecture but it is safe to assume that no money is changing hands.

32. The female Trick of great beauty can be readily identified by her habit of putting a cigarette in her mouth with an attitude of absolute assurance that someone else will light it.

33. It might appear to the casual observer that wives are Tricks. This betrays a sorry lack of perception, since no word as innately lighthearted as Trick could ever be used to describe someone with whom you share a joint checking account.

34. It is not good form to take a Trick out unless one is so firmly established as to be able to afford being associated with someone who might at any given moment write a poem in public.

35. Tricks are often plenteous gift givers. Upon receiving such offerings, one does well to

forget old adages, for while it may certainly be true that good things come in small packages it must not be forgotten that this is also the case with ceramic jewelry.

36. Letters from female Tricks are immediately recognizable, as these girls are greatly inclined to cross their sevens and dot their *i*'s with little circles. In all probability this is caused by their associating the presence of a writing implement in their hand with the playing of tic-tac-toe.

> "There is a Talmudic saying," smiled Dr. Frumpfausen..."as follows. In choosing a friend, ascend a step. In choosing a wife, descend a step. When Froggie-would-a-wooing-go, when Froggie is you, my dear boy, he must step *down*, as many steps as there are beneath him— even unto the last!..."
>
> —*The Apes of God,*
> Wyndham Lewis

37. Tricks are distinctly susceptible to the allure of faraway places. If you reside in the Village they want to breakfast at the Plaza. If you live in Murray Hill it's Chinatown they long for. But no matter where you make your home, they all share a consuming desire to ride, in the middle of the night, the Staten Island Ferry. They will, without exception, consider your rejection of such a proposal cold and unfeeling, little realizing that you are simply protecting them from what you know would be overwhelming temptation were you ever to find yourself standing behind them on a moving boat.

SCIENCE

Science is not a pretty thing. It is unpleasantly proportioned, outlandishly attired, and often overeager. What, then, is the appeal of science? What accounts for its popularity? And who gave it its start?

In order to better understand the modern penchant for science it is necessary to take the historical point of view. Upon doing this, one makes the discovery that the further back one goes the less science one is likely to find. And that the science one does encounter is of a consistently higher quality. For example, in studying the science of yesteryear one comes upon such interesting notions as gravity, electricity, and the roundness of the earth—while an examination of more recent phenomena shows a strong trend toward spray cheese, stretch denim, and the Moog synthesizer.

These data unquestionably support my theory that modern science was largely conceived of as an answer to the servant problem and that it is generally practiced by those who lack a flair for conversation.

It is therefore not surprising that only after Abolition did science begin to display its most unsavory features. Inventions and discoveries became progressively less desirable as it became harder and harder to get good help.

Prior to the advent of this unfortunate situation the scientist was chiefly concerned with the theoretical. His needs properly attended to, he quite rightly saw no reason to disturb others by finding a practical application for his new-found knowledge. This resulted in the establishment of schools of thought rather than schools of computer programming. That this was a much pleasanter state of affairs than presently exists is indisputable, and one has only to look around to see that the unseemliness of modern science is basically the product of men whose peevish reactions to household disorder drove them to folly. Even in those cases where a practical touch was indicated one notes a tendency toward excess.

A typical example of this syndrome is Thomas Edison. Edison invented the electric light bulb, the purpose of which was to make it possible for one to read at night. A great and admirable achievement and one that would undoubtedly have earned him a permanent place in the hearts and minds of civilized men had he not then turned around and invented the phonograph. This single act led to the eventual furnishing of small apartments with quadrophonic sound systems, thereby making it impossible for the better element to properly enjoy his *good* invention. If one follows this line of thought to its logical conclusion one clearly sees that almost

without exception every displeasing aspect of
science is, in one way or another, a hideous
corruption of the concept of reading at night.
Reading is not a particularly popular pastime—
hence the warm welcome the majority of the
population has extended to such things as
snowmobiles, tape decks, and citizen band radios.
That these newer appliances have not entirely
taken away the appetite of the public for electric
lamps can only be attributed to their unwilling-
ness to let perfectly good empty sangria bottles
go to waste.

Scientists are rarely to be counted among the
fun people. Awkward at parties, shy with
strangers, deficient in irony—they have had no
choice but to turn their attention to the close
study of everyday objects. They have had ample
opportunity to do so and on occasion have been
rewarded with gratifying insights.

Thus electricity was the product of Franklin's
interest in lightning, the concept of gravity the
outcome of Newton's experience with an apple,
and the steam engine the result of Watt's
observation of a teakettle.

It is only to be expected that people of this sort
are not often invited out. After all, a person who
might well spend an entire evening staring at a
kitchen utensil has little to recommend him as a
dinner companion. It is far too risky—
particularly if the person in question is moved to
share his thoughts with others. Physical laws are
not amusing. Mathematical symbols do not
readily lend themselves to the double entendre.

Chemical properties are seldom cause for levity. These facts make it intolerable for a gathering ever to include more than one scientist. If it is unavoidable, a scientist may be safely invited to dinner providing that he is absolutely the only member of his profession present. More than one scientist at the table is bad luck—not to mention bad taste. Legend has it that the atom was split when a bunch of scientists working late decided to order in a pizza. Indeed a terrifying story and one made all the more chilling when one learns that a number of their colleagues smarting from the snub of being excluded from this impromptu meal spitefully repaired to an all-night diner and invented polyester.

The Nail Bank:
Not Just Another Clip Joint

During a recent luncheon with a practicing
member of the leisure class the subject of
fingernail care chanced (as it so often does) to
come up. My companion chided me for what she
considered to be the disgraceful condition of my
fingernails and suggested quite strongly that I
accompany her to the inordinately tony establishment that is responsible for the impeccable
condition of her own. Upon learning the cost of
such an outing I curled my upper lip in an
attractive yet forceful manner and declined her
invitation with little regret. I was, however,
helpless against the demands of my constantly
questing mind and felt compelled to inquire as to
what exactly could be done to fingernails to
warrant such expense. "Why," replied my friend,
"they shape them, they wrap them, they polish
them, and if I need it they give me a transplant."
"A transplant," I repeated. "What do you mean, a
transplant?"

"Well, if I break a nail and I have the broken
piece they put it back on. But if I don't they use
someone else's nail from the nail bank." "The nail
bank?" I repeated again.

"Yes," she said and began to explain further,

but I must confess that I was no longer listening, for I was far too intent on my own imaginings. I left the table in a daze and remember little of the hours that followed, since my mind was reeling with vivid nail bank visions. I have finally managed to get some sort of grip on this thing and here is how it works:

Every year there is a nail drive. Volunteer nail workers set up shop in such likely establishments as finishing schools, health clubs, secretarial pools, and Henri Bendel's. The donor enters the room set aside for this purpose, lies down on a portable Ultrasuede chaise longue, and extends her hands. The volunteer nail worker carefully clips three nails from each hand (any more would be dangerous; any less, uncharitable) and then offers the donor a glass of Knox gelatine so that she may regain her strength. The nails are then placed in sterile containers and rushed to the nail bank. There they are typed accordingly:

    Type O—Oval
    Type A—Angular
    Type B—Bent, slightly
    Rh negative—Right hand, out of the question

When the victim of a broken nail is brought into the salon a team of dedicated manicurists matches the victim's type with the specimens on hand and performs the transplant with meticulous skill. There are, however, frequent shortages and it is not uncommon for a victim to wait days for a compatible type. Measures, of course, have been taken to alleviate this situation.

During the annual nail drive volunteers comb the city in an effort to convince those girls too selfish to donate in life to do so in death. These girls carry upon their persons cards that in the event of their demise instruct the authorities to clip so that another might receive the gift of renewed length. When one of these girls meets with a fatal accident that miraculously leaves her nails intact, a manicurist is raced to the scene and the procedure is carried out with dignity and dispatch.

Now, it sometimes happens that there are two girls in need of the same type nail but only one such nail is available. In a case like this the nail properly goes to the better tipper, but occasionally both girls are equally matched in this department. When this occurs the girls are brought before a judicial body known formally as the Emery Board. The Emery Board is composed of four experts in the field: a hairdresser, a headwaiter, a doorman, and Another Woman. The board members ask the girls the following pertinent questions:

1. Where are you going this evening?
2. With whom?
3. Wearing what?

The girls are then asked to leave the room while the judges confer. More often than not a decision is reached based upon the answers to the board's questions, but from time to time there is a deadlock. In such a circumstance the girls are not without recourse, for they can then turn to the Court of Appeal. The Court of Appeal is presided over by a temperamental photographer and a dictatorial fashion editor. The Court of Appeal is a visual rather than a verbal institution and favorable judgments are awarded solely on the basis of polish. Decisions of the Court of Appeal are final. Recently, however, it was discovered that the judges had ruled against a girl who lived on Beekman Place in favor of one who resided in the West Seventies. The judges were understandably relieved when this decision was overturned, for they, too, are firm believers in that wise old adage: Nothing succeeds like address.

Digital Clocks and Pocket Calculators:
Spoilers of Youth

I was in certain respects a rather precocious youngster. My glance, right from the start, was fraught with significance and I was unquestionably the first child on my block to use the word *indisposed* in a sentence. My childhood was not, however, quite the gay whirl that one might imagine from the above statements. As a whistler I was only fair and I am to this very day unable to assume even a humane attitude in regard to gerbils. But then as now, I was always capable of dealing with the larger issues—it was, and is, the little things that get me down.

I did not learn how to tell time until I was nine years old. This is an unusually advanced age at which to master the art, except perhaps in Southern California.

My parents were understandably upset about my inability to tell time, for they possessed the foresight to realize that any child who talked back with such verve and snap would one day need a lawyer who charged by the hour. Furthermore, their infinite wisdom told them that it was exceedingly unlikely that the bill would arrive reading: Consultation on contract with agent, $150.00. One and one-half hours. From big hand on twelve, little hand on three, to little hand on four, big hand on six.

Their concern for my future well-being drove them to frantic efforts in an attempt to instill in me the knowledge that so painfully eluded my grasp. Night after night I sat at the kitchen table and surveyed a bewildering array of clocks made from oatmeal cookies, peanut butter lids, and crayoned circles of colored paper. They spelled each other—first one parent and then the other—taking turns on watch, so to speak. They were diligent, patient, and kind and I nodded my head and looked alert, all the while seething with fury at the injustices of a world in which we didn't have Christmas but we did have Time. As the days wore on and my ignorance persisted, my parents toyed with the idea of renting me out as a parlor game or at least trading me in for a child who couldn't learn something else—so weary were they of round, flattish objects.

Outside intervention came in the form of an offer of help from my aunt to take me on for the week of my winter vacation. I was duly dispatched to Poughkeepsie, where I was alternately bribed with banana milk shakes and tortured with clocks devised from paper plates, circular throw pillows, and overturned frying pans. At the end of the week I was returned to my parents a thing that was once a child—as ever unable to tell time and newly addicted to banana milk shakes in a household that considered blenders frivolous.

Some months later I was taking a bath when I

suddenly shouted "Eureka!" and at long last such
concepts as twenty of eight and ten after twelve
were touched with meaning.

It should be readily apparent to all that under
no circumstances will I ever consider yielding the
need for such hard-won knowledge. That there
does indeed exist the very real danger of such a
possibility is entirely due to the invention of the
digital clock. I spent the best years of my life
learning to tell time and I'm not stopping now.
Neither should you. Here's why:

1. Regular clocks tell real time. Real time is
   time such as half-past seven.
2. Digital clocks tell fake time. Fake time is time
   such as nine-seventeen.
3. Nine-seventeen is fake time because the
   only people who ever have to know that it's
   nine-seventeen are men who drive subway
   trains.
4. I am not a man who drives a subway train.
5. You are not a man who drives a subway
   train.
6. I can tell this without even seeing you
   because anyone who has to know that it's
   nine-seventeen cannot possibly risk looking
   away.
7. Real watch faces are in the shape of watch
   faces because they must accommodate all of
   the things that make up a real watch, such as
   numbers, hands, and little minute lines.
8. Digital watch faces are in the shape of watch
   faces for no apparent reason. This cannot
   help but have an unsettling effect upon the
   young.

Now that I have set the record straight on the matter of Time I should like to direct your attention briefly to another unacceptable invention:

Pocket Calculators: It Took Me Three Years to Learn How to Do Long Division and So Should They

1. The rigors of learning how to do long division have been a traditional part of childhood, just like learning to smoke. In fact, as far as I am concerned, the two go hand in hand. Any child who cannot do long division by himself does not deserve to smoke. I am really quite a nice girl and very fond of children but I do have my standards. I have never taught a child to smoke before he has first taken a piece of paper and a pencil and demonstrated to my satisfaction that he can correctly divide 163 by 12.

2. Pocket calculators are not inexpensive and, generally speaking, parents would be better off spending the money on themselves. If they *must* throw it away on their offspring they would do well to keep in mind that a pack of cigarettes rarely costs more than seventy-five cents.

3. It is unnatural for *anyone*, let alone a *child*, to be able under any circumstances whatsoever to divide 17.3 by 945.8.

4. Pocket calculators encourage children to think that they have all the answers. If this belief were actually to take hold they might well seize power, which would undoubtedly result in all of the furniture being much too small.

A Final Word

I am not personally a parent. But I do have two
godchildren and am expecting a third. I am
naturally concerned for their future. If I ruled the
world you could bet your boots that none of them
would ever set their eyes on any such contrap-
tions as digital clocks and pocket calculators. But
alas, I do not rule the world and that, I am afraid,
is the story of my life—always a godmother,
never a God.

Weak Speech Handsets:
Aid for the Dull

The average person reacts to the arrival of his phone bill with a simple snort of disgust, but I frequently find my displeasure tempered with a touch of anticipation. For, unpleasant as it is to receive the written proof that one has indeed been whiling away the slender remainder of one's youth in costly, idle chat, one is nevertheless helpless against the fact that one is inordinately fond of a good long read. And quite fortunate that is; for the phone bills that I receive are not the sort of phone bills one glances at—they are the sort of phone bills one leafs through.

While recently perusing such a document my attention was immediately captured by two rather jarring particulars. The first being that although I had spent the lion's share of the month not at home, my bill was thick with calls to expensive parts of the nation. I mulled this over and decided that this irregularity could be easily explained if one was willing to accept the possibility that a heroin addict well connected in the movie business had periodically broken into my apartment and called Beverly Hills. I accepted, without reservation, just such a possibility. The second attention-getter was an item that appeared on the back of page eight, where I discovered a list of special phones available to the discriminating caller:

1. Trimline
2. Princess
3. Bell Chime
4. Tone Ringer
5. Volume Control Handset
6. Weak Speech Handset

I had a brief flirtation with Bell Chime and a frivolous dalliance with Tone Ringer, but my heart was won by Weak Speech Handset.

I considered momentarily the possibility that the Weak Speech Handset had been designed for those who had suffered some unfortunate incident of the throat but quickly discarded the notion that the phone company was capable of such realism. I cast about for a likely theory and hit upon the following.

The Weak Speech Handset is aimed at the tedious crowd—those who are weak in the speech department. This device takes the wearisome remarks of the boring and converts them into sparkling repartee. There is no question but that such an invention is long overdue. It is, however, quite unlikely that its usefulness will be much recognized by those who need it most. It is probable, then, that Weak Speech Handsets will be largely purchased as gifts. And perhaps therein lies a certain justice; undoubtedly the listener will derive the greatest benefits. For one cannot help but assume that if the caller was as aware of his ennui-inducing qualities as was the callee, he would stop talking entirely and concentrate on his personal appearance.

Believing strongly that variety is the spice of life, I have thoughtfully prepared a catalog detailing a wide selection of models from which to choose.

The Oscar Wilde

Produces speech that is entirely epigrammatic. . . . You will fool no one, but in certain small sections of the country you will be very popular . . . in certain other sections of the country you will be arrested. . . . A great favorite among consenting adults . . . available only in yellow.

The Dorothy Parker

A sarcasm lover's delight . . . particularly efficient at making humorous remarks on the subject of suicide. . . . Order now and receive as a free bonus an attractive round table.

The Gore Vidal

A bit higher priced but you will profit in hours of rib-tickling fun. . . . Fully equipped with self-transformer. . . . dispenses once and for all with

the need for two phones...perfect for Him *and*
Her.

The Evelyn Waugh

Thrill and amaze your loved one...the
ultimate in contempt...a must for those with a
taste for the trenchant.

The Alexander Pope

A sure-fire hit with heroic-couplet buffs
...especially entertaining in matters pertaining
to hair.

The Primary Cause of Heterosexuality Among Males in Urban Areas: Yet Another Crackpot Theory

The most commonly heard complaint among heterosexual women in New York concerns the dearth of heterosexual men. Should you hear such talk you would be well advised to direct the complainant to a Soho bar. For here she would be surrounded by such a plethora of eager gents that she might well wonder just who's buying all those plaid flannel shirts. Why, she may ask, is this particular quarter of the city so heavily populated by young men to whom the name Ronald Firbank means nothing? To this query there can be only one reply—heterosexuality among males in urban areas is caused primarily by overcrowding in artist colonies. This is a scientific fact. Here is how we know.

Scientists observed over a long period of time the behavior of a group of twenty rats living in an apartment with high ceilings and working fireplaces. All twenty rats were artists. All twenty rats were, as is normal in such cases, homosexual. Five of these rats were chosen at random and taken in a knapsack to West Broadway, where they were moved into a loft. They were joined there by ninety-five other rats who were also homosexual artists and had also

been chosen at random from a number of other
natural habitats such as doorman buildings and
converted brownstones. All hundred rats had,
when in their proper environments, exhibited
absolutely no inclination toward unusual sexual
behavior. Once, however, faced with life in a
neighborhood that contained so many galleries
and so few decent restaurants, an alarming
pattern began to emerge. First they stopped
painting and started having concepts. Then they
began consuming a diet heavy in raisins and the
less expensive but heartier red wines. Finally,
many of them displayed a decided tendency to
teach two days a week at the School of Visual
Arts. Once this occurred they were past the point
of no return and began seeking the company of
female rats who had gone to Bennington in the
late sixties.

The scientists, understandably horrified by
the results of their tampering with the natural
order, tried to stem the rising tide of heterosexuality by appealing to the rats' greatest weakness.
They chose a small group of rats who had
previously been the most hard-core of the S & M
crowd. They led them over to the docks on the
Hudson River. Here they attempted to stir old
fires by tossing into the murky waters those
accoutrements most cherished before the move
to Soho. First they let dangle and then drop a
black leather cap with metal ornaments. The rats
responded with agitated tail movements but
stayed put. Next they tried a pair of rugged boots
complete with menacing-looking spurs. Still no

action. Finally the scientists threw into the river a long, snaky leather whip. Their spirits lifted as several of the rats scurried to the edge of the dock. But instinct was overcome by conditioning, and they watched with heavy hearts and defeated eyes the rats desert the sinking whip.

Why I Love Sleep

I love sleep because it is both pleasant and safe to use. Pleasant because one is in the best possible company and safe because sleep is the consummate protection against the unseemliness that is the invariable consequence of being awake. What you don't know won't hurt you. Sleep is death without the responsibility.

The danger, of course, is that sleep appears to be rather addictive. Many find that they cannot do without it and will go to great lengths to ensure its possession. Such people have been known to neglect home, hearth, and even publishers' deadlines in the crazed pursuit of their objective. I must confess that I, too, am a sleeper and until quite recently was riddled with guilt because of it. But then I considered the subject more carefully and what I learned not only relieved my guilt but also made me proud to be among the fatigued.

I would like to share my findings so that others might feel free to lay down their once uplifted heads. I have therefore prepared a brief course of instruction in order to instill pride in those who sleep.

The Fran Lebowitz Sleep Studies Program

Sleep is a genetic rather than an acquired trait. If your parents were sleepers, chances are that you will be too. This is not cause for despair but rather for pride in a heritage that you share not only with your family but also with a fine group of well-known historical figures. The following list is indicative of the diversity to be found among sleepers:

Some Well-known Historical Figures Who Were Sleepers

Dwight D. Eisenhower

While many remember Ike (as he was affectionately called by an adoring nation) for his golf, there is little doubt but that he was a sleeper from childhood, a trait he unquestionably carried with him to the White House. In fact, so strongly committed was he to sleep that one could barely distinguish Ike's sleeping from Ike's waking.

William Shakespeare

Known as the Bard among his colleagues in the word game, Shakespeare was undoubtedly one of literature's most inspired and prolific sleepers. Proof of this exists in the form of a bed found in the house he occupied in Stratford-upon-Avon. Further references to sleeping have been discovered in his work, and although there is some question as to whether he actually did all his own sleeping (scholarly debate currently centers around the possibility that some of it was done by Sir Francis Bacon), we are nevertheless safe in assuming that William Shakespeare was indeed a sleeper of note.

e. e. cummings

The evidence that e. e. cummings was a sleeper is admittedly sparse. Therefore, it is generally accepted that he was perhaps more of a napper.

It is only to be expected that if so many well-known historical figures were sleepers, their accomplishments should be of equal import. Following is a partial list of such achievements:

Some Contributions to World Culture Made by Sleepers

> Architecture
> Language
> Science
> The wheel
> Fire

I rest my case.

Good Weather and Its Propensity to Frequent the Better Neighborhoods

It was once the common belief that the climate was determined by a large number of gods, each in charge of a specific variety of weather. Then came the major religions, and most people came to hold a more subdued point of view that suggested but a single god who got around a lot. Many still take this position, although the majority now ascribe to a theory of weather based largely on cloud formation, air pressure, wind velocity, and other aspects of science. Lastly, there are those who feel that the weather and what it does are entirely the province of honey-throated television announcers with big Magic Markers. So, then, we are presented with three basic theories as regards the controlling factor of weather:

A. God
B. Nature
C. Tone of Voice

To the casual observer it would appear that these three theories are widely disparate. That, of course, is the problem with casual observers. Their very casualness—that trait we once all found so attractive...so appealing...so devil-may-care—is precisely what makes them so quick to judge and therefore so frequently inaccurate. The more vigilant observer would unquestioningly be able to detect a rather striking similarity. That similarity being that all three theories are based quite simply on mere whim—God can change his mind, Nature can change her course, and Voice, as we all know only too well, can change its tone.

Thus we find that by and large the world considers weather to be something, if not all, of a romantic—given to dashing about hither and yon raining and snowing and cooling and heating with a capriciousness astonishing if not downright ridiculous in one so mature. Well, the world may think what it bloody well likes but I for one will have nothing to do with such faulty logic and so have formulated what I believe to be a more reasonable theory.

"Why," I asked myself, "should the weather be any different from you or me—are we not all one?" When presented with a question of such startling clarity I was compelled to answer, "No reason, Fran, no reason at all." "Well then," I continued, "it follows that if weather is no different from you or me, then it must be the same as you or me, in which case that which controls *us* must control *it*." "Can't argue with that," I replied, realizing with a start that I was in the presence of a master. "And what," I queried further, "do you think that is? Only one thing—money. That's right, money." "When you're right you're right," was the welcome reply, and with that my companion and I strode off happily hand in hand—a gesture which, while it did lend us a certain September Mornish aspect, was in no way unattractive.

While some may find this argument specious, I offer the following as absolute definitive evidence that it is money and money alone that influences the weather.

1. On August 13, 1975, at 3:00 P.M., the temperature on Fourteenth Street and Eighth Avenue was ninety-four degrees—the humidity 85 percent. On the exact same date and at the exact same time the temperature on Seventy-third Street and Fifth Avenue was a balmy seventy-one degrees—the humidity a comfortable 40 percent. I know, because I was there.

2. The only recorded instance of rain on Sutton Place occurred when a scene from a big-budget movie was being shot in the vicinity and the script called for inclement weather. The moment the powerful Hollywood director yelled "Cut!" the rain stopped.

3. The reason that then mayor John Lindsay did not send snowplows to Queens during that much publicized blizzard was that he lived on Gracie Square, where on the day in question he was lying on his terrace taking the sun.

4. It is widely believed that in the summer rich people leave New York to go to Southampton because the weather is cooler there. This is not true. What actually happens is that in the summer the cooler weather leaves New York and goes to Southampton because it doesn't

want to stay in New York with a lot of underpaid
writers and Puerto Ricans.

5. Generally speaking, the weather is better
on the East Side than on the West Side. All in all,
the weather considered this arrangement satisfactory except for the problem posed by the
better buildings on Central Park West. The
problem was solved by means of a trade-off with
certain buildings in the East Seventies that are
largely populated by beyond-their-means airline
stewardesses and the proprietors of leather
boutiques. Thus the San Remo and the Dakota
receive weather appropriate to their architecture and airline stewardesses and the proprietors of leather boutiques are perhaps those
among us who must fully understand the
meaning of the term "fair-weather friend."

Plants: The Roots of All Evil

The Unabridged Second Edition of Webster's Dictionary—a volume of no small repute—gives the following as the second definition of the word *plant:* "any living thing that cannot move voluntarily, has no sense organs and generally makes its own food. . . ." I have chosen the second definition in favor of the first because it better serves my purpose, which is to prove once and for all that, except in extremely rare instances, a plant is really not the sort of thing that one ought to have around the house. That this might be accomplished in an orderly manner, I have elected to consider each aspect of the above definition individually. Let us begin at the beginning:

Any Living Thing

In furnishing one's place of residence one seeks to acquire those things which will provide the utmost in beauty, comfort, and usefulness. In the beauty department one is invariably drawn to such fixtures as Cocteau drawings, Ming vases, and Aubusson rugs. Comfort is, of course, assured by the ability to possess these objects.

Usefulness is something best left to those trained in such matters.

It should, then, be apparent that at no time does Any Living Thing enter the picture except in the past tense. In other words, it is perfectly acceptable to surround oneself with objects composed of that which while alive may have been Any Living Thing but in death has achieved dignity by becoming a nice white linen sheet.

That Cannot Move Voluntarily

Here one is confronted with the problem that arises when Any Living Thing takes the form of an extra person. An extra person is quite simply a person other than oneself. Living things of this nature undoubtedly have their place in both town and country, as they usually prove to be the most adept at typing, kissing, and conversing in an amusing fashion. It must be pointed out, however, that moving voluntarily is the very key to their success in performing these functions; the necessity of having to actually operate them would quite eliminate their appeal.

I have previously stated my contention that plants are acceptable in extremely rare instances. This type of extremely rare instance occurs when one is presented with a leaf-ridden token of affection by an extra person who has provided valuable service. Refusal of a plant thus offered will almost certainly result in the termination of this bond. Therefore, while the decision as to who exactly should be allowed to burden one with such a memento is, of course, a matter of personal conscience, one is wise to remember that talk is cheap, a kiss is just a kiss, but manuscripts do not type themselves.

Has No Sense Organs

It is necessary to remember that, although No Sense Organs does most assuredly guarantee no meaningful glances, no snorting derisively, and no little tastes, it also, alas, guarantees no listening spellbound.

And Generally Makes Its Own Food

There is, I believe, something just the tiniest bit smug in that statement. And Generally Makes Its Own Food, does it? Well, bully for It. I do not generally make my own food, nor do I apologize for it in the least. New York City is fairly bristling with restaurants of every description and I cannot help but assume that they are there for a reason. Furthermore, it is hard to cherish the notion of a cuisine based on photosynthesis. Thus, since I have yet to detect the aroma of Fettuccine Alfredo emanating from a Boston fern, I do not consider And Generally Makes Its Own Food to be a trait of any consequence whatsoever. When you run across one that Generally Makes Its Own Money, give me a call.

Mars: Living in a Small Way

Not too long ago the United States succeeded in landing on Mars an unmanned spacecraft, the chief purpose of which was to ascertain whether or not anyone lives there. The results are not all in yet but there is, I am afraid, little doubt that the answer will be in the affirmative. It is pointless to assume that the earth alone is afflicted with the phenomenon of life.

There has been a good deal of speculation as to the personal appearance of these foreigners and much has been made of the possibility that this life might be of such exotic aspect that we here at home would be unable to recognize it. An interesting thought indeed, but, alas, like all interesting thoughts it has at its core the basest sort of longing. For as an earthling who has seen, if not it all, then at least all that I care to, I cannot help but be reminded of that immutable truth: if you go looking for trouble you're bound to find it.

Under the impression that life makes itself evident only in the physical mode, the general public—a perenially lackluster bunch—tends to dwell on such matters as arms, noses, and neck size, thereby envisioning a being that differs from the average Joe only in the most superficial detail. Scientists—a crowd that when it comes to style and dash makes the general public look like the Bloomsbury Set—seem to speak largely of microbes, gases, and liquid states.

This concern with the corporeal is really superfluous. There is, of course, life on Mars and we shall, of course, recognize it, if not by its form, then most certainly by its function, which it undoubtedly shares with our own local brand of life: the will to annoy.

In order to recognize *which is life* we must first deal with the somewhat broader question of *what is life*. Here we discover that others have preceded us and provided quite a range of answers. We consider each answer individually but we are invariably disappointed. A bowl of cherries? Too pat. A cabaret? Not in this neighborhood. Real? Hardly. Earnest? Please.

It is by this painstaking method of careful examination and eventual rejection that we reach a conclusion: life is something to do when you can't get to sleep. Therefore, that which we call civilization is merely the accumulated debris of a chilling number of bad nights.

There is no reason to believe that the Martians are any less nervous than we are (indeed they are very likely more so—their insomnia compounded by the problems of living so far uptown) and therefore they are undoubtedly a thoroughly unpleasant lot.

Let us assume for the purposes of this essay that the Martians are microbes. Microbes are undeniably on the small side, which means that basketball and fashion models are definitely not in the picture. Such deficiency in size is worthy of comment, for the concept of an entire planet that cannot reach the top shelf is seriously disconcerting. Perhaps we can best understand these beings by a careful study of Mars as a whole.

Mars

It is generally accepted that Mars was named for the Roman god of war. This is erroneous. The closely guarded truth is that it was actually discovered by a Roman gentleman of artistic temperament who attempted to use his achievement to romantic advantage. The Roman, his eye on an attractive but elusive Swedish fellow, tried flattery. Great political pressure was brought to bear and he eventually came to understand that the Roman Empire had no intention of allowing any planet of theirs to be called Lars. As you can see, a compromise was reached.

The Land and Its Resources

Mars is the third smallest planet and therefore of interest only to collectors. It is bleak and rocky with no coastline to speak of—a feature that has made it one of the few beach areas within the financial grasp of this writer. Finding a taxi is next to impossible and visitors are advised not to.

Natural resources run heavily to alien vapors and strange stones.

The People and Their Work

The people, as has been stated before, are microbes—a condition that makes them at best peoplettes and at worst microbes. Their work consists mainly of getting visitors to stop making jokes about their height.

Population

This is difficult to determine unless one is prepared to look at the situation very closely.

Transportation

The favored mode of transportation is infecting a visitor and then hoping that he goes someplace.

Chief Products

The chief products of Mars are tiny little polyester leisure suits and miniature graduate schools.

City Limiting:
The New Geography

I had barely recovered from the appellative blow struck by SoHo (*So*uth of *Ho*uston Street) when I received a quick left to the sensibility in the form of NoHo (*No*rth of *Ho*uston Street). Head bloody but unbowed, I dropped my guard and TriBeCa (*Tri*angle *Be*low *Ca*nal Street) scored a T.K.O. in the very first sound.

I have been laid up now for quite a while and have had ample time to consider this matter in detail. Yes indeed, I've given this thing a lot of thought and I've come to the conclusion that this crazed naming of extremely specific areas of the city has yet to come to full flower. An appalling situation—no end in sight—there is not the slightest indication that these area buffs have named their last. It is abundantly clear that such vague terms as Midtown will no longer suffice; it will only get worse and will probably go something like this:

NoTifSoSher

NoTifSoSher (*No*rth of *Tif*fany's, *So*uth of the *Sher*ry-Netherland) is a two-block stretch of Fifth Avenue much favored by shoppers, hotel guests, and strollers from all walks of life. Its attractive jewelry displays and one-way traffic have made it one of the most desirable locations in the city. The undisputed king of the parade route, NoTifSoSher is beloved by Irishmen and war veterans alike. A must-see for taxi-hailers.

BeJelfth

A little-known section of town, BeJelfth is a whimsically placed block of West Fourth Street (*Between* Jane and Tw*elfth*). Truly a cabby stumper, BeJelfth is a favorite meeting place for dogs both large and small. The delicatessen on the corner is a veritable Mecca for thrill-seekers who never fail to be amazed by the dizzingly skyrocketing prices.

Little Humility

Long a bastion of male camaraderie, this eccentrically shaped area is bounded on the east by the beginning of Christopher Street and on the west by the Hudson River. Although positively reeking with unconventional charm, Little Humility is a snap to find as it deviates not an inch from the beaten path and abounds with cunning little bars and irresistible tractor-trailer trucks. Those who frequent this district have every right (and every left) to refer to it proudly as the Keys to the City.

Food for Thought
and Vice Versa

Summer has an unfortunate effect upon hostesses who have been unduly influenced by the photography of Irving Penn and take the season as a cue to serve dinners of astonishingly meager proportions. These they call light, a quality which while most assuredly welcome in comedies, cotton shirts, and hearts, is not an appropriate touch at dinner.

It is not surprising that a number of such hostesses seem to be associated with the world of high fashion, for it follows that a person whose idea of a hard day's work is posing for Deborah Turbeville might also be of the opinion that parsley is an adequate meat course.

Thin, almost transparent slices of lemon do indeed go a long way in dressing up a meal but they should not be counted as a separate vegetable.

*　*　*

Cold soup is a very tricky thing and it is the rare hostess who can carry it off. More often than not the dinner guest is left with the impression that had he only come a little earlier he could have gotten it while it was still hot.

* * *

A salad is not a meal. It is a style.

* * *

Japanese food is very pretty and undoubtedly a suitable cuisine in Japan, which is largely populated by people of below average size. Hostesses hell-bent on serving such food to occidentals would be well advised to supplement it with something more substantial and to keep in mind that almost everybody likes french fries.

* * *

Vegetables are interesting but lack a sense of purpose when unaccompanied by a good cut of meat.

* * *

Water chestnuts are supposed to go in a thing, not to be the thing itself.

* * *

White grapes are very attractive but when it comes to dessert people generally like cake with icing.

* * *

Candied violets are the Necco Wafers of the overbred.

There are a number of restaurants in New York that cater primarily to the confirmed bachelor. These establishments share many characteristics with the summer hostess and then some.

One such local eatery is a remodeled diner that looks like what Busby Berkeley would have done if only he hadn't had the money. It is open twenty-four hours a day—one supposes as a convenience to the hungry truck driver who will belly up to the takeout counter and bellow, "Two cucumber soups—good and cold; one endive salad—red wine vinaigrette; and one order of fresh asparagus—hold the hollandaise."

Saffron should be used sparingly if at all. No matter how enamored one might be of this seasoning, there are few who would agree that it is equal to salt in the versatility department.

* * *

A native-born American who has spent the entire day in what he knows to be New York City and has not once stepped aboard a ship or plane is almost invariably chagrined and disoriented by a menu that uses the French counterpart for the perfectly adequate English word *grapefruit*.

* * *

Watercress is pleasant enough in a salad or sandwich, but when placed alongside a hamburger it is merely an annoyance.

* * *

While it is undeniably true that people love a surprise, it is equally true that they are seldom pleased to suddenly and without warning happen upon a series of prunes in what they took to be a normal loin of pork.

* * *

People have been cooking and eating for

thousands of years, so if you are the very first to have thought of adding fresh lime juice to scalloped potatoes try to understand that there must be a reason for this.

Technological innovation has done great damage not only to reading habits but also to eating habits. Food is now available in such unpleasant forms that one frequently finds smoking between courses to be an aid to the digestion.

A loaf of bread that is more comfortable than a sofa cannot help but be unpalatable.

* * *

The servant problem being what it is, one would think it apparent that a society that provides a Helper for tuna but compels a writer to pack her own suitcases desperately needs to reorder its priorities.

* * *

Chocolate is an excellent flavor for ice cream but both unreasonable and disconcerting in chewing gum.

* * *

Breakfast cereals that come in the same colors as polyester leisure suits make oversleeping a virtue.

* * *

When one asks for cream one should receive either cream or the information that the establishment in question favors instead a combination of vegetable oil and cancer-causing initials.

* * *

Cheese that is required by law to append the word *food* to its title does not go well with red wine or fruit.

Thoroughly distasteful as synthetic foods might be, one cannot help but accord them a certain value when confronted with the health food buff. One is also ever mindful of the fact that the aficionado of whole foods is a frequent champion of excessive political causes.

* * *

Brown rice is ponderous, overly chewy, and possessed of unpleasant religious overtones.

* * *

Civilized adults do not take apple juice with dinner.

* * *

Inhabitants of underdeveloped nations and victims of natural disasters are the only people who have ever been happy to see soybeans.

* * *

Bread that must be sliced with an ax is bread that is too nourishing.

* * *

Large, naked, raw carrots are acceptable as food only to those who live in hutches eagerly awaiting Easter.

* * *

Food is such a common occurrence in our daily lives that few have taken the time to consider it in the broader sense and thus cannot truly appreciate its impact on society.

Food is welcome at both meal and snack time. It goes well with most any beverage and by and large makes the best sandwich.

* * *

Food gives real meaning to dining room furniture.

* * *

Food goes a long way in rounding out a CARE package.

* * *

Food offers the perfect excuse to use the good dishes.

* * *

Food is an important part of a balanced diet.

* * *

Food plays a crucial role in international politics. If there was no such thing as food, state dinners would be replaced by state bridge games and, instead of fasting, political activists would probably just whine.

* * *

A foodless world would have the disastrous effect of robbing one's initiative. Ambition has no place in a society that refuses its members the opportunity to become top banana.

* * *

Without food, one of man's most perplexing yet engaging problems would be rendered meaningless when one realized that the chicken and the egg both didn't come first.

*   *   *

If food did not exist it would be well-nigh impossible to get certain types off the phone, as one would be unable to say, "Look, I've got to run but let's have dinner sometime soon."

*   *   *

Food was a very big factor in Christianity. What would the miracle of the loaves and fishes have been without it? And the Last Supper—how effective would that have been?

*   *   *

If there was no such thing as food, Oyster Bay would be called just Bay, and for the title of *The Cherry Orchard*, Chekhov would have chosen *A Group of Empty Trees, Regularly Spaced.*

ARTS

Perhaps the least cheering statement ever made on the subject of art is that life imitates it. This would doubtless be more heartening news were its veracity not quite so capricious. For upon inspection it is immediately apparent that life is at its most artistic when such a condition is least desired. It is, in fact, safe to assume that, more often than not, life imitates craft, for who among us can say that our experience does not more closely resemble a macramé plant holder than it does a painting by Seurat. When it comes to art, life is the biggest copycat in the matter of the frame.

Wishing to investigate the matter more thoroughly, I gathered about me a group of like-minded associates and began the long, hard work of imitating art in its most contemporary manifestations.

Conceptual Art

We positioned ourselves randomly on a hardwood floor and pretended to be cinder blocks. We affixed to our shirtfronts labels bearing words unrelated to one another in a linear sense. We were not understood and we were greatly admired. We found this to be not unfulfilling.

Graphic Design

Some of us dressed up like bold, daring lines; others, like large, clear, easy-to-read letters and numbers. All of us wore simple yet childish bright colors. We arranged ourselves in the shape of an airport and adopted a manner both useful and sprightly. We were most popular with those similarly dressed.

Magazine Layout

Quite a few of us wore the same things we had worn when following the example of Graphic Design, although we went to considerably smaller sizes. The rest of us divided ourselves equally into two groups—one being airbrushed color illustration; the other being out-of-context, blown-up quotations from articles. All of us stationed ourselves for maximum intrusion value. Everyone crowded together in the form of a single page but kept our distance by the clever use of numerous black borders. We were a big hit and proved once and for all that you can take the art out of art direction but you can't take the direction out of art, at least not if it's headed that way.

Furniture Design

We researched this one carefully and decided to be both fun and functional. We wore molded plastic, durable fabrics, and lots of butcher's block. We assumed the shapes of gigantic bean bags, inflatable rafts, hard-edged paintings, and cumulus clouds. We were rather reminded of our days as Graphic Design and felt more than ever that we had a multi-purpose in life.

Architecture

We thought a lot about glass and new, lightweight building materials. We imagined ourselves schools, shopping centers, office buildings, public housing, and luxury apartment complexes. We hoped that at least a few of the others would imagine themselves signs so that people could tell us apart.

Popular Music

We attired ourselves in shiny garments so as to accurately reflect the hopes and dreams of the general public. We entered elevators, cars, planes, telephones, and just about every place else you couldn't think of. We were an inescapable influence on the culture and inspired a fanatical devotion, for we made a joyful noise unto the bored.

Movies

We were careful to adopt only those attitudes associated with work of serious intention, being well aware that life generally does not imitate entertainment. We exhibited extreme sensitivity and technical prowess while motioning lyrically. We explored the themes of violence, despair, and social injustice that lurk beneath the slick surface of our society. We were nice and quiet, saying little and keeping pretty much to ourselves.

Fashion

Some of us borrowed quite heavily from others. Some of us were unduly imaginative. A lot of us felt silly making these statements but we attempted to invest them with deeper meaning. This was not, in light of the preponderance of polyester, easy, but people bought it. Believing us to be expressions of their true personalities, the public clasped us to their bosoms and added a few fun touches of their own.

Not in the: Mood Jewelry

As one whose taste in mental states has always run largely toward the coma, I have very little patience with the current craze for self-awareness. I am already far too well acquainted with how I feel and frankly, given the choice, I would not. Anyone who is troubled by the inability to feel his or her own feelings is more than welcome to feel mine. It should not be surprising, then, for you to learn that I am something less than enchanted with a concept such as mood jewelry. For those of you fortunate enough to have your lack of awareness extend into the realm of advertising, mood jewelry is jewelry that tells you your feelings via a heat-sensitive stone. And although one would think that stones would have quite enough to do, what with graves and walls and such, it seems that they have now taken on the job of informing people that they are nervous. And although one would think that a person who is nervous would be more than able to ascertain that fact without the aid of a quite unattractive ring, this is apparently not the case.

Mood jewelry comes to us in many guises: necklaces, rings, watches, and bracelets. But whatever form it takes, it is invariably equipped with the perceptive and informative stone that not only relates one's present mood but also indicates in what direction that mood is headed. The stone performs this newsy feat by means of color change. The following, chosen solely on the basis of crankiness, has been excerpted from an ad:

EACH COLOR CHANGE REVEALS THE INNER YOU!

ONYX BLACK...Overworked.

AMBER RED...You are becoming more strained, even anxious.

TOPAZ YELLOW...Somewhat unsettled, your mind is wandering.

JADE GREEN...Normal, nothing unusual is happening.

TURQUOISE BLUE-GREEN...You are beginning to relax...your emotions are turning up.

LAPIS BLUE...You feel comfortable...you belong. Relax...your feelings are beginning to flow freely.

SAPPHIRE BLUE...You're completely open ...feeling happy...concentrating on your strong inner feelings and passions. This is the highest state.

One can safely assume that a person who finds it necessary to consult a bracelet on the subject of his own state of mind is a person who is undoubtedly perplexed by a great many things. It follows, then, that in such a case a piece of jewelry that reveals only emotions can hardly be called adequate—for here is a person besieged and beset by questions far more complex than "Am I strained?" This is an individual who needs *answers*—an individual who should be able to look at his heavily adorned wrist and ask, "Am I tall? Short? A natural blond? A man? A woman? An elm? Do I own my own home? Can I take a joke? Do I envy the success of others?"

Clearly, if there is to be such a thing as mood jewelry it must become more specific. In the interests of hastening such an occurrence I offer the following:

THE FRAN LEBOWITZ GUIDE
TO EVEN GREATER SELF-TRUTHS THROUGH

REDDISH BEIGE...You are an American Indian who is boring...you are of little interest both to yourself and to other American Indians.

BEIGISH RED...You are a white person who is boring...you are deeply embarrassed by your complete lack of interesting qualities...humility is no substitute for a good personality...this will not change.

LAVENDER...You are either a homosexual or a bathroom rug in a house where you match the tile...if you decide in favor of being a bathroom rug just remember that as a homosexual you could have been on the David Susskind Show.

HORIZONTAL STRIPES...You are extremely thin and have reacted to this fact excessively...this is the lowest state.

MULATTO...One of your parents is turning into a Negro...if your parents are already Negroes one of them is turning into a white person.

IRREGULAR, FINE LINES...You are getting somewhat older...this will probably continue.

BURNT UMBER...You are turning into an artist...possibly Hans Holbein, the Younger. This is the highest state.

Clothes with Pictures
and/or Writing on Them:
Yes—Another Complaint

Now, I'm not just talking about Vuitton bags. Or Gucci wallets. Or Hermès scarves. Designers and/or business concerns who splash their names and initials all over overpriced accoutrements of dubious quality are of course sorely lacking in taste, but I am not going to be sidetracked by trivialities. I'm talking about the larger issues. Open-necked Deco-ish shirts with a repeating pattern of middle-sized silhouettes of sailboats. Blue jeans depicting the death of Marilyn Monroe in waterproof pastels. Dresses upon which one (but preferably two) can play Monopoly. Overalls that remind toddlers, through the use of small pink animals spouting comic strip balloons, to brush their teeth. T-shirts that proclaim the illegal sexual preferences of the wearer. Etcetera. Etcetera.

While clothes with pictures and/or writing on them are not entirely an invention of the modern age, they are an unpleasant indication of the general state of things. The particular general state of things that I am referring to is the general state of things that encourages people to express themselves through their clothing. Frankly, I for one would not be unhappy if most people expressed themselves by marching en masse into the nearest large body of water but, barring that, I wish they would at least stop attempting to tell all by word of jacket. I mean, be realistic. If people don't want to listen to *you*, what makes you think they want to hear from your sweater?

There are two main reasons why we wear clothes. First, to hide figure flaws, of which the average person has at least seventeen. And second, to look cute, which is at least cheering. If some people think that nice, muted solid colors are a bit dull they can add some punch with stripes, plaids, checks, or—if it's summer and they're girls—small dots. And for those of you who feel that this is too restrictive, answer me this: If God meant for people to walk around in coats that have pictures of butterscotch sundaes on them, then why does *he* wear Tattersall shirts?

Soho: Or Not at Home
with Mr. Art

Soho is a real place. By real I mean that it exists materially. Mr. Art is not a real person. By not a real person I mean that he does not exist materially. Nevertheless, where Soho is concerned I wouldn't consider excluding Mr. Art from my observations, for in matters such as this he is my most trusted adviser and confidant. He is a dapper little fellow, perhaps a bit wry—and while it has been said of him that his manner cannot really support his mannerisms, he is, I can assure you, a welcome relief from some of these other types we get in here.

I will introduce you to Soho slowly by noting that this area of downtown Manhattan shares with Mr. Art nary a single characteristic. Up until a few years ago Soho was an obscure district of lofts used chiefly for storage and light manufacturing. It wasn't called Soho then—it wasn't called anything because no one ever went there except the people who make Christmas tree ornaments out of styrofoam and glitter or fabric trimmings out of highly colored stretch felt. And say what you will about members of these professions, they are generally, I am sure, very nice people who not only don't make those things out of choice but also don't go around calling obscure districts of Manhattan things like Soho. Ostensibly, Soho is called Soho because it begins *South* of *Houston* Street, but if you want my opinion I wouldn't be too terribly surprised to discover that the person who thought up this name is a person whose circle of friends in 1967 included at least one too many English photographer. It was, of course, a combination of many unattractive things that led to the Soho of today, but quite definitely the paramount factor was the advent of Big Art. Before Big Art came along, painters lived, as God undoubtedly intended them to, in garrets or remodeled carriage houses, and painted paintings of a reasonable size. A painting of a reasonable size is a painting that one can easily hang over a sofa. If a painting cannot be easily hung over a sofa it is obviously a painting painted by a painter who got too big for his brushes and is in fact the very sort of painting responsible for Mr. Art's chronically curled upper lip. Painters, however, are not the only ones involved here. Modern sculptors, or *those chiselers* as Mr. Art is wont to call them, must bear a good part of the blame, for when clay and marble went out and demolished tractor-trailer trucks came in, Big Art was here to stay.

One day a Big Artist realized that if he took all of the sewing machines and bales of rags out of a three-thousand-square-foot loft and put in a bathroom and kitchen he would be able to live and make Big Art in the same place. He was quickly followed by other Big Artists and they by Big Lawyers, Big Boutique Owners, and Big Rich Kids. Soon there was a Soho and it was positively awash in hardwood floors, talked-to plants, indoor swings, enormous record collections, hiking boots, Conceptual Artists, video communes, Art book stores, Art grocery stores, Art restaurants, Art bars, Art galleries, and boutiques selling tie-dyed raincoats, macramé flower pots, and Art Deco salad plates.

Since the beginning of the Soho of today the only people in New York who have been able to get through a Saturday afternoon without someone calling them on the telephone to suggest that they go down to Soho and look at the Art are those who belong to Black Nationalist organizations. As neither myself nor Mr. Art is a member of such a group, we consider it quite a feather in our mutual cap that we have succumbed to these ofttimes strongly worded suggestions so infrequently, and that on the rare occasions that we have we certainly have not been gracious about it.

A recent Saturday was just such an occasion and here is what we saw:

Art Gallery Number One

A girl who would probably have been a welcome addition to the teaching staff of any progressive nursery school in the country had

instead taken it upon herself to create out of
ceramic clay exact replicas of such leather objects
as shoes, boots, suitcases, and belts. There was
no question but that she had achieved her goal—
one had literally to snap one's fingernail against
each object and hear it ring before one was
convinced that what one was snapping one's
fingernail against was indeed ceramic clay and
not leather. And one could, of course, choose to
ignore Mr. Art as he hissed, "Why bother?" and
struck a match across a pair of gloves in order to
light one of his aromatic foreign cigarettes.

Art Gallery Number Two

A young man who had apparently been
refused admission to the Boy Scouts on moral
grounds had arranged on a shiny oak floor
several groups of rocks. He had then murdered a
number of adolescent birch trees in order to bend
them into vaguely circular shapes and hang them
on the wall. These things were all for sale at
prices that climbed well into the thousands. "First
of all, imagine actually wanting to *own* any of this
stuff," sneered Mr. Art, "and then imagine not
being able to figure out that with an ax and a
wheelbarrow you could make it all yourself in a
single morning and still have time to talk to your
plants."

Art Gallery Number Three

Two boys who were really good friends had taken a trip to North Africa. They took a lot of color photographs of bowls, skies, pipes, animals, water, and each other. They had arranged the photographs alphabetically—i.e., A—Ashes, B—Bright sunny day—pasted them to pieces of varnished plywood, written intricately simple little explanations beneath each photograph, and hung them under their appropriate letters. I am compelled to admit that upon viewing this work Mr. Art had to be forcibly restrained from doing bodily harm to himself and those around him.

Art Gallery Number Four

Someone who had spent a deservedly lonely childhood in movie theaters had gotten hold of a lot of stills from forties films, cut out the faces of the stars, hand-colored them, and pasted them to blow-ups of picture postcards from Hollywood and Las Vegas. "Too camp," said Mr. Art testily upon being awakened; "they oughta lock 'em all up."

Art Galleries Number Five Through Sixteen

Scores of nine-by-twelve photo-realist renderings of gas stations, refrigerators, pieces of

cherry pie, art collectors, diners, '59 Chevys, and
Mediterranean-style dining room sets.

Mr. Art and I are presently seeking member-
ship in a Black Nationalist organization. In the
meantime we have taken our phone off the hook.

Color: Drawing the Line

Color is, of course, not wholly without virtue. Shape being insufficient, it is necessary that things possess a certain measure of color in order that they might be distinguished one from the other. It would hardly do if in reaching for a cigarette one picked up a pen and discovered that the prospect of a moment's relaxation had turned instead into hours of tedious labor. It is, however, doubtful in the extreme that the degree of color demanded by simple distinction bears any relation whatsoever to such a concept as lime green.

I am not, I assure you, totally unreceptive to color providing it makes its appearance quietly, deferentially, and without undue fanfare. I am compelled to make this statement in view of the current popular belief that color is capable of conveying ideas and supplying us with a key to the human personality. This type of thing has become far too prevalent and I for one absolutely and unequivocally refuse to be bullied about by a thing's capacity to absorb light. There is nothing less appealing than a color fraught with meaning—the very notion is boisterous, inappropriate, and marked by the dreariest sort of longing.

Due to the urgent nature of this situation it is necessary that purely aesthetic considerations be allied with the equally grave concerns of philosophical error. The entire matter has too long been ignored—a hue and cry are long overdue.

The Primary Colors

The primary colors are the most blatantly abused. Chief offenders can be divided into two main camps.

First, the graphic design crowd who think that primary colors are both cheering and bold and demonstrate this belief by employing them incessantly in places where people have every right to be depressed. In fact, so widespread is the use of red, yellow, and blue in schools, airports, and cancer hospitals that, should one find oneself with neither textbook nor luggage in a place thus adorned, one could not be accused of overreacting were one to decide to jump.

Second, there are those who endeavor too stridently to impart an aura of passion, childlike innocence, or serenity, depending upon which primary color they have chosen. The concern here is, of course, not with those who use these colors moderately but rather with those who, lacking the personality to get carried away with themselves, are forced instead to get carried away with someone else.

Red

Red is frequently associated with passion because it is the color of fire. Those who take this seriously need to be reminded that there is such a thing as arson.

Yellow

People who favor yellow with inordinate gusto are attempting to create an air of childlike innocence and sunny optimism. As these particular properties cannot possibly be the reason for the color of warning signals and legal pads, one would be well advised to look both ways before crossing.

Blue

Blue is supposed to indicate serenity because it is the supposed color of water, which is supposedly a calm and restful element. In dealing with champions of this hue one could do worse than remember that water is also the favorite environment of sharks and the cause, nine times out of nine, of death by drowning.

The Secondary Colors

The secondary colors—green, orange, and

purple—are merely variations on a theme. They, like the primary colors, have their place and are often, I am told, found in nature.

Despite all this I remain, where color is concerned, less than enthusiastic. There are those who contend that without it the world would be a very dull place indeed—and then again there are those who contend that at least it wouldn't clash.

The Sound of Music:
Enough Already

First off, I want to say that as far as I am concerned, in instances where I have not personally and deliberately sought it out, the only difference between music and Muzak is the spelling. Pablo Casals practicing across the hall with the door open—being trapped in an elevator, the ceiling of which is broadcasting "Parsley, Sage, Rosemary, and Thyme"—it's all the same to me. Harsh words? Perhaps. But then again these are not gentle times we live in. And they are being made no more gentle by this incessant melody that was once real life.

There was a time when music knew its place. No longer. Possibly this is not music's fault. It may be that music fell in with a bad crowd and lost its sense of common decency. I am willing to consider this. I am willing even to try and help. I would like to do my bit to set music straight in order that it might shape up and leave the mainstream of society. The first thing that music must understand is that there are two kinds of music—good music and bad music. Good music is music that I want to hear. Bad music is music that I don't want to hear.

So that music might more clearly see the error

of its ways I offer the following. If you are music
and you recognize yourself on this list, you are
bad music.

1. Music in Other People's Clock Radios

There are times when I find myself spending
the night in the home of another. Frequently the
other is in a more reasonable line of work than I
and must arise at a specific hour. Ofttimes
the other, unbeknownst to me, manipulates an
appliance in such a way that I am awakened by
Stevie Wonder. On such occasions I announce
that if I wished to be awakened by Stevie Wonder
I would sleep with Stevie Wonder. I do not,
however, wish to be awakened by Stevie Wonder
and that is why God invented alarm clocks.
Sometimes the other realizes that I am right.
Sometimes the other does not. And that is why
God invented *many* others.

2. Music Residing in the Hold Buttons of Other People's Business Telephones

I do not under any circumstances enjoy hold
buttons. But I am a woman of reason. I can accept
reality. I can face the facts. What I cannot face is
the music. Just as there are two kinds of music—
good and bad—so there are two kinds of hold
buttons—good and bad. Good hold buttons are
hold buttons that hold one silently. Bad hold

buttons are hold buttons that hold one musically. When I hold I want to hold silently. That is the way it was meant to be, for that is what God was talking about when he said, "Forever hold your peace." He would have added, "and quiet," but he thought you were smarter.

3. Music in the Streets

The past few years have seen a steady increase in the number of people playing music in the streets. The past few years have also seen a steady increase in the number of malignant diseases. Are these two facts related? One wonders. But even if they are not—and, as I have pointed out, one cannot be sure—music in the streets has definitely taken its toll. For it is at the very least disorienting. When one is walking down Fifth Avenue, one does not expect to hear a string quartet playing a Strauss waltz. What one expects to hear while walking down Fifth Avenue is traffic. When one does indeed hear a string quartet playing a Strauss waltz while one is walking down Fifth Avenue, one is apt to become confused and imagine that one is not walking down Fifth Avenue at all but rather that one has somehow wound up in Old Vienna. Should one imagine that one is in Old Vienna one is likely to become quite upset when one realizes that in Old Vienna there is no sale at Charles Jourdan. And that is why when I walk down Fifth Avenue I want to hear traffic.

4. Music in the Movies

I'm not talking about musicals. Musicals are movies that warn you by saying, "Lots of music here. Take it or leave it." I'm talking about regular movies that extend no such courtesy but allow unsuspecting people to come to see them and then assault them with a barrage of unasked-for tunes. There are two major offenders in this category: black movies and movies set in the fifties. Both types of movies are afflicted with the same misconception. They don't know that movies are supposed to be movies. They think that movies are supposed to be records with pictures. They have failed to understand that if God had wanted records to have pictures, he would not have invented television.

5. Music in Public Places Such as Restaurants, Supermarkets, Hotel Lobbies, Airports, Etc.

When I am in any of the above-mentioned places I am not there to hear music. I am there for whatever reason is appropriate to the respective place. I am no more interested in hearing "Mack the Knife" while waiting for the shuttle to Boston than someone sitting ringside at the Sands Hotel is interested in being forced to choose between sixteen varieties of cottage cheese. If God had meant for everything to happen at once, he would not have invented desk calendars.

Epilogue

Some people talk to themselves. Some people sing to themselves. Is one group better than the other? Did not God create all people equal? Yes, God created all people equal. Only to some he gave the ability to make up their own words.

A Brush with Death

Perhaps one of the more noteworthy trends of our time is the occupation of buildings accompanied by the taking of hostages. The perpetrators of these deeds are generally motivated by political grievance, social injustice, and the deeply felt desire to see how they look on TV. They are a bold lot—reckless and driven—true champions of equal time.

Although repeatedly in the news, these events were more often than not ignored in artistic circles. This element was unconcerned and felt far removed from such occurrences, lacking as they were in visual impact. Their complacency was, however, rudely shattered by a series of incidents that stunned the art world with their daring use of local color and imposing command of space.

Incident No. 1—"Untitled" (Gasoline on Rag)

A small band of exiled Cubists took over the Great Rotunda in the Capitol Building in Washington, D.C., and threatened to set it on fire unless the entire city was broken down into its

basic geometric forms. They took as hostages
Three Musicians and announced to the media
that unless their demands were met the violinist
would be forced at gunpoint to, in the words of
Braque X, the leader of the group, "fiddle while
domes burned."

Desperate to avoid such a tragedy, government officials conferred through the night, and
on the following morning an Abstract Expressionist was sent in to negotiate a peaceful
settlement. The Abstract Expressionist, a crafty
fellow with a long history of pulling the wool
over people's eyes, seemed to be making some
headway until Braque X accused him of having
no perspective on the subject. This delayed the
proceedings for hours but eventually the Abstract Expressionist, who had every reason to
want the Cubists out of the picture, calmed
Braque X by guaranteeing safe passage if he
promised to give up his crazy scheme. Braque X,
realizing that they had him up against the wall,
accepted the offer and an assemblage of planes
and angles transported the Cubists back to their
rightful place in art history.

The police, however, were not satisfied with
the outcome and the commanding officer, with a
hard edge to his voice, declared in an interview,
"My five-year-old daughter could do better than
that." This opinion captured the imagination of
the public and a vigilante committee was quickly
formed. Late that night the Abstract Expressionist was escorted by a firing squad out into the

middle of a color field and splattered with bullets—another victim of shifting tastes.

Incident No. 2—"Girl with Submachine Gun"

A group of feminist artists known as Women Against took hostage a group of male representational painters and demanded to know why they depicted women as having breasts. The men answered that they painted women with breasts because women had breasts, and accused the feminists of fear of framing. The women instantly saw the wisdom of this and apologized profusely, explaining that they were severely depressed because they were all having their Blue Period.

Incident No. 3—"Form Following a Function"

The good eye of the whole world was upon a small Italian town when a revolutionary terrorist organization known as the Bauhaus Bombers threatened to turn the Leaning Tower of Pisa into a machine for dying by blowing it up. Intent on avoiding clutter, the Bauhaus Bombers took no hostages but demanded instead that one purely decorative object be destroyed every hour on the hour until their goal was achieved. Just what this goal was, was not known, for they insisted upon secrecy unless proof could be shown that no other terrorist organization had designs on it. Fearing the loss of the historic building, officials acquiesced totally. Truckloads of bric-a-brac were brought into the town square. Under the direction of the Bombers, dozens and dozens of china figurines, clever wall hangings, and superfluous vases were sacrificed to the mysterious cause.

Time went on and still the terrorists refused to divulge their purpose. Daily the crowds grew more restive and the police, faced with the possibility of a riot, finally devised a plan of action. By dressing one of their number in rust-colored wide-wale corduroy and a black turtle-neck sweater, they managed to infiltrate the organization. In due time intelligence reached them that the arsenal they had envisioned was instead one mere bomb of exceedingly meager proportions. Astonished that the Bombers would equip themselves so minimally, they questioned their agent as to the reason for this folly. Having spent a good deal of time in the tower he simply looked at them coolly and remarked, "Less is more."

Much relieved, the police entered the building and easily overcame their adversaries. Once in custody the Bauhaus Bombers spoke freely, maintaining passionately that their cause was just. All they wanted, they said, was for the Leaning Tower of Pisa to be straightened out. Asked why such extreme measures had been taken, they shouted, "Never again!" They then leveled their final and unarguable charge against the sinking edifice: that the Leaning Tower of

Pisa was and continues to be blatantly anti-symmetric.

Incident No. 4—"Reclining Chair and Toaster Eating Licorice"

A small but incongruous group of the followers of Dada known as MOMA all dressed in pants and went to the outskirts of Chicago. They then sent a message to the President of the United States demanding a more amusing juxtaposition of laws. Before the President could respond, a well-known consumer advocate charged the members of MOMA with lining a teacup with the pelt of an endangered species. The Dadaists were brought before a Senate subcommittee and forced to accept the terms of an agreement that would compel them in the future to use fun fur or none at all. The members of MOMA bridled at this restriction, as synthetic fabrics had already taken their toll by rendering an iron with nails in it far less witty than was orginally thought. Looking back in retrospect, the Senate strictures were a blessing in disguise, enabling the Dadaists to realize that they had invented a form that lent itself to museums—which thereby lifted their spirits and gave them all a good laugh.

Incident No. 5—"

A frightening number of conceptual artists (two) occupied space in downtown Manhattan and, when no one noticed, were obliged to go uptown. There they arranged some rocks in a pattern that announced that they were holding hostage one hundred and sixty-eight videotape cassettes. They demanded that people imagine that this was of any interest. When no response was forthcoming they congratulated themselves heartily on their success and repeated the action endlessly.

LETTERS

Owing to the conditions that currently prevail in the world of letters, it is now possible for a girl to be ruined by a book. Owing, in fact, to the conditions that currently prevail in the world of letters, it is now possible for a boy to be ruined by a book.

A book, of course, is not the only danger, for things have come to such a pass that a magazine is safer than a book only to the extent that it is shorter. But magazines all too frequently lead to books and should be regarded by the prudent as the heavy petting of literature.

This warning should be heeded by all concerned, and in order to bring about a less perilous printed environment, I offer the following tips on how to avoid the reading and/or writing of ruinous material.

Women's Books

Enroll in medical school and specialize in gynecology. It will not be long before disenchantment sets in and you realize that the literary possibilities of the vulva have been somewhat overestimated.

* * *

Women who insist upon having the same options as men would do well to consider the option of being the strong, silent type.

* * *

Having been unpopular in high school is not just cause for book publication.

* * *

Having been popular in high school should have been enough. Do not share this experience with the reading public.

* * *

If your sexual fantasies were truly of interest to others, they would no longer be fantasies.

* * *

As an aficionado of literature it might interest you to know that, in all of Shakespeare, the word *assertive* appears not a single time.

* * *

Keep in mind that there are still certain subjects that are unsuitable at the table, and that a great many people read while eating.

Poetry

If you are of the opinion that the contemplation of suicide is sufficient evidence of a poetic nature, do not forget that actions speak louder than words.

*   *   *

Generally speaking, it is inhumane to detain a fleeting insight.

*   *   *

The free lunch was originated by saloonkeepers during the Depression. Free verse also often originates during depression. If this happens to you, try to nip it in the bud by taking a drink.

*   *   *

If, while watching the sun set on a used-car lot in Los Angeles, you are struck by the parallels between this image and the inevitable fate of humanity, do not, under any circumstances, write it down.

Special-Interest Magazines

Being a woman is of special interest only to aspiring male transsexuals. To actual women, it is simply a good excuse not to play football.

*   *   *

Special-interest publications should realize that if they are attracting enough advertising and readers to make a profit, the interest is not so special.

*   *   *

The exchange of information concerning the

whereabouts of the best down comforter or chicken tandoori in New York should, I guess, be permitted between consenting adults in private so long as the young and the literate are left unmolested.

* * *

Sexual congress with heavy machinery is not a special interest. It is a personality defect.

Self-Help Books

There is no such word as *actualize*. There is no such word as *internalize*. There is, in fact, but one instance where the letters *ize* are appropriate here and that is in the word *fertilize*.

* * *

Mental health is rarely, if ever, achieved by reliving your birth in a bathtub.

* * *

If you want to get ahead in this world, get a lawyer—not a book.

* * *

Wealth and power are much more likely to be the result of breeding than they are of reading.

* * *

While it may occasionally occur that one's character shows in one's face, this is nothing to count on, for one's face will show in one's character long before that possibility has had a chance to arise.

WRITING: A LIFE SENTENCE

Contrary to what many of you might imagine, a career in letters is not without its drawbacks—chief among them the unpleasant fact that one is frequently called upon to actually sit down and write. This demand is peculiar to the profession and, as such, galling, for it is a constant reminder to the writer that he is not now, nor will he ever really be, like other men. For the requirements of the trade are so unattractive, so not fair, and so foreign to regular people that the writer is to the real world what Esperanto is to the language world—funny, maybe, but not *that* funny. This being the case, I feel the time has come for all concerned to accept the writer's differences as inherent and acknowledge once and for all that in the land of the blind the one-eyed man is a writer and he's not too thrilled about it.

Thus I offer the following with the hope that it will bring about much-needed compassion. Points 1 through 5 are for parents—the later explication for masochists. Or vice versa.

How to Tell if Your Child Is a Writer

Your child is a writer if one or more of the following statements are applicable. Truthfulness is advised—no amount of fudging will alter the grim reality.

1. Prenatal

   A. You have morning sickness at night because the fetus finds it too distracting to work during the day.
   B. You develop a craving for answering services and typists.
   C. When your obstetrician applies his stethoscope to your abdomen he hears excuses.

2. Birth

   A. The baby is at least three weeks late because he had a lot of trouble with the ending.
   B. You are in labor for twenty-seven hours because the baby left everything until the last minute and spent an inordinate amount of time trying to grow his toes in a more interesting order.
   C. When the doctor spanks the baby the baby is not at all surprised.
   D. It is definitely a single birth because the baby has dismissed being twins as too obvious.

3. Infancy

   A. The baby refuses both breast and bottle,

preferring instead Perrier with a twist in preparation for giving up drinking.
B. The baby sleeps through the night almost immediately. Also through the day.
C. The baby's first words, uttered at the age of four days, are "Next week."
D. The baby uses teething as an excuse not to learn to gurgle.
E. The baby sucks his forefinger out of a firm conviction that the thumb's been done to death.

4. Toddlerhood

A. He rejects teddy bears as derivative.
B. He arranges his alphabet blocks so as to spell out derisive puns on the names of others.
C. When he is lonely he does not ask his mother for a baby brother or sister but rather for a protégé.
D. When he reaches the age of three he considers himself a trilogy.
E. His mother is afraid to remove his crayoned handiwork from the living room walls lest she be accused of excessive editing.
F. When he is read his bedtime story he makes sarcastic remarks about style.

5. Childhood

A. At age seven he begins to think about changing his name. Also his sex.
B. He balks at going to summer camp because he is aware that there may be children there who have never heard of him.
C. He tells his teachers that he didn't do his

homework because he was blocked.

D. He refuses to learn how to write a Friendly Letter because he knows he never will.

E. With an eye to a possible movie deal, he insists upon changing the title of his composition "What I Did on My Summer Vacation" to the far snappier "Vacation."

F. He is thoroughly hypochondriac and is convinced that his chicken pox is really leprosy.

G. On Halloween he goes out trick-or-treating dressed as Harold Acton.

By the time this unfortunate child has reached puberty there is no longer any hope that he will outgrow being a writer and become something more appealing—like a kidnap victim. The concern, then, as he enters the difficult period of adolescence, is that he receive the proper education in a sympathetic environment. For this reason it is strongly recommended that the teen writer attend a school geared to his dilemma—Writing High. At Writing High the student will be among his own kind—the ungrateful. He will be offered a broad range of subjects relevant to his needs: Beginning Badly, Avoiding Los Angeles One and Too, Remedial Wakefulness, Magazine Editors: Why?, and Advanced Deftness of Phrase—all taught by jealous teachers who would really rather be students. Extracurricular activities (such as the Jacket Flap Club, where students have fun while learning the rudiments of acquiring colorful temporary jobs such as lumberjack, numbers runner, shepherd, and pornographer) are in plentiful supply. The figure of speech team, the Metaphors, are mighty effective. They can mix it up with the best of them, and Janet Flanner, their lovable mascot, is a great campus favorite.

Although the yearbook—*The Contempt*—is rarely finished in time for graduation, it is nevertheless a treasured memento of the years spent at Writing High. The cafeteria is presided over by an overweight woman of great ambition and serves mediocre Italian food at ridiculously inflated prices. School spirit is encouraged by holding in the auditorium a weekly gathering known as Asimile. Tutoring is available for the slow student, or "ghost," as he is referred to at Writing High. Upon graduation or expulsion (and expulsion is favored by the more commercial students, who prize it for its terrific possibilities as a talk-show anecdote) the writer is as ready as he'll ever be to make his mark upon the world.

It is unnecessary to detail the next, or actual career, stage, for all writers end up the same— either dead or in Homes for the Aged Writer. The prospect of being put in such an establishment is viewed by all writers with great dread and not without reason. Recent scandals have revealed the shockingly widespread sadistic practice of slipping the aged writer unfavorable reviews, and more than one such victim has been found dead from lack of sufficient praise.

Not a very pretty picture, I'm afraid, and not a very accurate one either. But don't be encouraged by *that*—two wrongs don't make you write.

IN HOT PURSUIT

There recently appeared in the *New York Post* an article concerning the sexual abuse and exploitation of several thousand young boys in the Los Angeles area. Hard facts were on the sparse side but the police department did make some estimates:

> More than 3,000 children under the age of fourteen are being exploited sexually in the Los Angeles area.

> At least 2,000 local adult males actively pursue boys under the age of fourteen.

> More than 25,000 juveniles from fourteen to seventeen years of age are used sexually by approximately 15,000 adult males.

I was, of course, surprised to see so many numbers on a list of what were admittedly allegations and wondered just where they had gotten their figures. It was difficult to imagine the police actually going around counting, so instead I imagined this:

A Study in Harlots

In thinking back on the many exhilarating and arduous adventures that I have shared with my friend Mr. Sherlock Homes and Gardens, I can recall none more perplexing (or more fun) than that which I have chosen to call *A Study in Harlots*. Of course, *The Case of Dom Pérignon 1966* presented its problems, *The Afghan Hound of the Baskervilles* was hardly easy, and *The Baker Street Extremely Irregulars* was no piece of chicken, but none was a match for the tale I now tell.

First, allow me to introduce myself. I am Dr. John Watson, although Homes and Gardens often refers to me simply as "my dear." I am a qualified physician with a limited practice in the East Sixties (right near Halston's) and, I must say, much in demand, for between my own work and my association with Homes and Gardens it is generally acknowledged that Dr. John Watson knows exactly where all the bodies are buried. Homes and Gardens and I dwelt, of course, for many years at 221-B Baker Street, but the plummeting pound and outrageous taxes drove us from London, just as it did Mick, Liz, and so many other of our friends. We have taken up residence in Manhattan at an excellent address between Park and Madison (right near Halston's) and it is here that our story begins.

It was approximately eleven o'clock on a pleasant morning in early December when I descended the staircase of our tastefully appointed duplex penthouse. Homes and Gardens, an earlier riser than I, had already breakfasted and was lying, eyes closed, on the damask-covered Empire Récamier. Edward, a very attractive young man whose acquaintance we had recently made, played Homes and Gardens's violin for him. Homes and Gardens used, of course, to play his own violin, but that was before we made it. Homes and Gardens stretched a languid hand in greeting, his well-cut silk Saint Laurent shirt-sleeve in graceful folds around his wrist, and said, "Watson, my dear, I see that you are a bit weary after your long evening in which you first attended a cocktail party in honor of Bill Blass's new sheet collection, had dinner at Pearl's with a number of fashion notables, drank brandy at Elaine's with a well-known author, danced at Regine's with a famous person's daughter, and then went downtown to do it with a stranger." I fell into a Louis XVI Marquise and looked at Homes and Gardens wonderingly, for all my years of being roommates with him had done nothing to diminish my astonishment at his remarkable powers of deduction. "How did you know?" I asked as soon as I had regained my composure. "I didn't see you at all yesterday, for you were busy being photographed for *L'Uomo Vogue* and I had no chance to tell you of my plans." "Elementary, my dear: The first four items I observed this morning in *Women's Wear Daily*, the last I deduced by noting that your indigo blue Jackie Rogers jacket is lying more smoothly than usual against your seriously white Viyella sweater, indicating that your somewhat recherché Fendi wallet is missing." My hand flew to my inside breast pocket but I knew it was futile, for Homes and Gardens was never wrong. "There, there, Watson my dear, no use getting into a snit about it—your wallet for a moment's pleasure is a rough trade, to be sure, but I think I have something that will take your mind off your loss. This morning there was a message on the service from Precious Little asking that we take the next flight to Los Angeles, as my assistance is required in a matter of no small delicacy."

Precious Little was an interesting fellow, though rather given to ancestor worship (other people's ancestors—he had none of his own to speak of) and Homes and Gardens had known him for years. His association with the Los Angeles Police Department was not exactly professional. He was not an officer of the law or even really a crime buff—it was, to be perfectly frank, quite simply that he had a most singular fondness for uniforms. Whatever his shortcomings, Precious was on the right side of the law and Homes and Gardens had aided him previously.

"Have our bags packed, my dear," said Homes and Gardens as he reached for the cocaine bottle, "I'll just do a few lines and then we must depart immediately." I made all haste and soon found myself sitting comfortably in the first-class compartment of a 747. A young woman in an ill-fitting pantsuit came to take our drink order.

Homes and Gardens looked at her keenly yet disdainfully and said, "Stolichnaya straight up—for I can see that you had a difficult time of it, what with the five whiskey sours you consumed before finally meeting that account executive, and the poor-quality but large quantity of marijuana that you smoked with the sales manager you ran into this morning when leaving the account executive's apartment in the East Seventies near Third Avenue." The young woman gasped in disbelief and stuttered, "But, sir—how did you—how did you . . . ?"

"Elementary," he said coolly, "all stewardesses are alike."

I chuckled appreciatively. Homes and Gardens turned to me and said, "Now, my dear, I will tell you all that Precious told me, so that you are prepared to observe me observing the situation. It seems that a certain captain in the Los Angeles Police Department, you know who I mean, has been giving estimates to the press about the number of people involved in an underage homosexual sex scandal. Precious feels (and not without reason) that the situation is being exaggerated—you know how our captain brags—and I have been asked to investigate the matter more thoroughly, for my way with a number is legend." "Yes indeed," I agreed, "they've certainly chosen the right man." Homes and Gardens lit his pipe and I sat back with a magazine. The rest of the flight was uneventful except for a slight altercation caused by some passengers who resented Homes and Gardens telling them how the movie ended before it even started ("Saw it at a screening last week," he confided to me triumphantly), but it was all soon settled and we arrived on schedule.

Precious Little had sent his matching car and driver and the ride to the hotel was a pleasant one. The Beverly Hills has in recent years lost a bit of its cachet, but Homes and Gardens is rather attached to its paging system and I myself am partial to its distinctive pink notepads.

No sooner had we settled into our bungalow (rather far from Halston's but right near the main building) than Precious himself arrived. "My Sher, my dear," he greeted us effusively and kissed us each on both cheeks, "you must come with me at once. That captain is becoming absolutely impossible. Daily his figures become more ridiculous and I have it from a very good source that he's hours away from talking to Rona."

"Well, well, Precious," said Homes and Gardens crisply, "that, of course, must be prevented, although it is unlikely, don't you think, that she'll take his call?" We all agreed and once more I was struck by Homes and Gardens's acute sensibilities.

The three of us got into the car—Homes and Gardens electing to sit up front, in order, he said, that he might see more clearly, although I imagine that what he wanted to see more clearly did not entirely exclude Juan, Precious's superbly café-au-lait driver. Homes and Gardens is, after all, a man of many interests.

We made an extensive tour of the various neighborhoods—Homes and Gardens gazing intently at every detail while Precious pointed out the homes of the stars. Our inspection completed, we repaired to Mr. Chow's, where we were welcomed extravagantly.

Precious and I looked at Homes and Gardens expectantly, but he avoided our eyes and I must confess that my heart sank as I allowed myself to feel for the very first time some doubt about my roommate. My spirits rose, however, when Homes and Gardens smiled precisely and said, "Oh, look, there's Liza, doesn't she look great?" I turned around and was pleased to see the celebrated entertainer waving cheerfully in our direction. We exchanged nods and turned our attention once again to Homes and Gardens, who was now obviously ready to address us.

"It's quite a simple thing really, reminds me in fact of the case involving the disappearance of a makeup artist at the *pret-à-porter* some years back. We knew for a fact that a makeup artist was missing—what we didn't know was just which makeup artist it was. Everyone, as you can imagine, was in a veritable tizzy, until I pointed out that we had only to examine the faces of the models, note which ones were most painfully lacking in cheekbone definition, inquire as to who did the makeup and thus we would have the name of the missing artist. From there the actual discovery of the young man took but a moment. Now, in the instance at hand, I must say we were most fortunate that the areas involved were not the very best, for had we been concerned with say, an area like Bel Air, we would have been confronted with the problem of ample household help. Since, however, we were dealing with such locales as Brentwood my work was quite trifling. You may have noticed, my dears, that I took much interest in the landscaping and I found exactly what I thought I would. A great many of the lawns were overgrown and needed cutting in the most dreadful way. I further learned that in many of the houses the garbage had not been taken out for days, nor had newspapers been delivered in quite some time. So many chores and part-time jobs left undone pointed to one thing and one thing only—that these neighborhoods were suffering from a dearth of underage boys. I simply counted up the amount of neglected work and can now present you with an accurate tally:

"1,582 children under the age of fourteen are being exploited sexually in the Los Angeles area. 1,584, to be exact, but the other two are movie stars, which is, I regret, not illegal.

"At least 10,000 local adult males actively pursue boys under the age of fourteen, but only 1,183 actually catch them.

"8,000 juveniles from fourteen to seventeen years of age are used sexually by approximately 14,000 adult males (rather slim pickings, that) but 28,561 adult males are used to far greater advantage by 19,500 very crafty juveniles, many claiming to be from fourteen to seventeen years of age."

Homes and Gardens sat back with a satisfied air and Precious Little and I congratulated him heartily. Once again Homes and Gardens's admirable talents had triumphed, and on the way out of the restaurant we saw Barbra and Jon snubbing Kris.

OR NOT CB:
THAT IS THE ANSWER

It was with considerable approval that I listened
one Sunday evening to my weekend host instruct
his chauffeur to drive us, his guests, back to New
York. The source of my approval was my firmly
held conviction that public transportation should
be avoided with precisely the same zeal that one
accords Herpes II. And, I must say, in view of my
slender means and broad acquaintance, I have on
the whole, been remarkably successful in escap-
ing both. It was, therefore, in excellent spirits
that I settled myself comfortably in the back seat
of the car. I smiled fondly at my companions, lit a
cigarette, and entered enthusiastically into a
discussion of the entertaining personal habits of
those not present. Under such circumstances it is
easily understandable that I did not, at first, pay
much attention to what I innocently believed to
be the harmless mutterings of the driver. It was
not until a silence, afforded by a lull in the
conversation, allowed me the opportunity of
genuine eavesdropping that I became aware that
someone was muttering back. I studied my fellow
passengers and was much relieved to conclude
that neither one had been concealing a secret
knowledge of ventriloquism. That the chauffeur

might possess such an intricate skill was quite out of the question. Overwhelmed by curiosity I asked him outright for an explanation. He replied that he was talking on the Citizen's Band radio he had recently installed in my host's automobile. The answering mutter was that of a truckdriver fifteen miles away. I asked him what he hoped to gain by this repartee. He replied that he was trading information on weather, traffic, and police radar cars.

I glanced out the window. It was a clear, starlit September evening. The traffic was bumper to bumper. If there was a police radar car in the vicinity it was probably reading the paper. I offered the chauffeur these observations. He responded by saying that he was finding out what the conditions were fifteen miles ahead of us. I replied that it was Sunday night, that we were on the Merritt Parkway bound for New York, and that ahead of us we would find the exact same conditions as those that currently prevailed except that they would become progressively more cosmopolitan. He ignored this news, preferring instead to resume his muttering. Seeing that this wasn't the first time I'd been thrown over for a truckdriver, I sat back to listen to what I imagined would be a distinctly lackluster conversation. What transpired, however, was unintelligible in a way I had not expected, for they spoke in a code that seemed totally devoid of meaning. This, I discovered, was CB slang—a special language used by those so inclined. As this was my first encounter with

Citizen's Band radio, I feel justified in having responded with mere distaste. I knew nothing about it. Now more than a year has passed. I know a lot about it. And yes, I am appalled—yes, I am horrified—and yes, I take issue.

I originally planned to take issue in the form of an exchange of letters between Oscar Wilde and Lord Alfred Douglas written in CB slang. I labored diligently but with little success, for CB slang as a means of communication is irretrievably butch. It is, in fact, safe to say that if the population of the United States was relieved entirely of its girls and its male homosexuals, CB slang would be English.

I am eminently qualified to make this statement, as I studied intensively for the aforementioned project. Thus I am confident in my contention that when it comes to CB slang I am virtually fluent. This surprises me—for I carry with me the memory of a youth fairly teeming with French tutors, all of whom eventually admitted defeat and announced that I had no ear for language. Perhaps, perhaps, but it matters not, for it turns out that when it comes to *lingo* I've got an ear and a half. Clearly, my linguistic ability was not the problem. I did what I could. I assigned to Lord Douglas the CB "handle" (or nickname) of "Jailbait." For Mr. Wilde I chose "Jailbird," thereby achieving an enviable symmetry. I read scores of their real letters. I ground away at the CB dictionary. I tried full translations. I tried partial translations. I tried footnotes. To no avail. CB slang is, after all, a limited tongue concerned primarily with four-car collisions, radar traps, shifting gears, and stopping for coffee. Mr. Wilde's and Lord Douglas's thoughts were elsewhere. There are, for instance, no CB equivalents for the words "gilt," "narcissus," "insouciance," or "honey-haired boy." And even the most perfect epigram suffers when interpreted in a language that refers to a bed as a "snore shelf."

Fortunately, I am a plucky sort and more than willing to express my displeasure in another manner:

The very word *citizen* implies a preoccupation with democracy that cannot help but be construed as fanatical. And not without reason, for entree to the world of CB is wide open to all and sundry—particularly all. It is harder, I assure you, to get into Macy's.

* * *

To the average (and you will look long and hard before finding anyone so aptly described) CB aficionado his radio is his hobby. A hobby is, of course, an abomination, as are all consuming interests and passions that do not lead directly to large, personal gain.

* * *

CB radio is a common bond. Any bond that cannot, upon demand of the bearer, be converted immediately into cash is sorely deficient in both refinement and dignity.

* * *

CB slang is on the one hand too colorful and on the other hand lacking a counterpart for the words *pearl gray*.

* * *

Citizen's Band radio renders one accessible to a wide variety of people from all walks of life. It should not be forgotten that all walks of life include conceptual artists, dry cleaners, and living poets.

* * *

CB communication consists almost wholly of actual information. It is, therefore, of no interest to the civilized conversationalist.

The Word *Lady:* Most Often Used to Describe Someone You Wouldn't Want to Talk to for Even Five Minutes

For years and years people who had them referred to their girl friends as their girl friends. With the advent of that unattractive style known as hip, many people stole the term *old lady* from perfectly innocent black jazz musicians and began using it in regard to their own girl friends. Then came women's lib and quite a number of people apparently felt that the word *old* was sexist. These people began to call their girl friends their "ladies."

Lest you get the impression that I am totally opposed to the word *lady* I rush to assure you that I think it is a perfectly nice word when used correctly. The word *lady* is used correctly only as follows:

A. To refer to certain female members of the aristocracy.
B. In reference to girls who stand behind lingerie counters in department stores, but only when preceded by the word *sales*.
C. To alert a member of the gentle sex to the fact that she is no longer playing with a full deck. As in, "Lady, what are you—nuts or something?"

D. To differentiate between girls who put out
   and girls who don't. Girls who put out are
   tramps. Girls who don't are ladies. This is,
   however, a rather archaic usage of the word.
   Should one of you boys happen upon a girl
   who doesn't put out, do not jump to the
   conclusion that you have found a lady. What
   you have probably found is a lesbian.

Taking a Letter

As one with a distinct aversion to newspapers I rely heavily for information on the random remarks of others. Therefore my sources are far from impeccable. They are, however, not without a peculiar whimsical charm all their own and thus not to be taken lightly. For example, I was recently informed that the United States Postal Service was considering cutting its deliveries down to three days a week. The informant was a source close to his mother and therefore reliable. My immediate reaction was one of shock and dismay until I remembered that in my neighborhood a week that sees three whole mail deliveries is a thing rare and precious. I began to wonder why it was that my local mail service was so far ahead of that of the rest of the nation and decided to make discreet inquiries.

My neighborhood is located in Greenwich Village, a quarter of the city well known for its interesting artistic qualities. These qualities are to be found not only in its atmosphere and residents but also in its public servants. There is, in fact, not a single local postal employee who does not possess a temperament of such lush moodiness that one assumes that only an

unfortunate lack of rhythm has kept them from
careers devoted to the composition of tragic
opera. Exhaustive research soon established that
this was no accident but a carefully planned
effort to bring the post office closer to those it
serves. The Greenwich Village Postal System is a
separate entity dedicated to the proposition that
nowhere on earth are men created more equal
than downtown on the West Side. Thus its
offices exhibit a clean Bauhaus influence. The
wanted posters refer to desires more personal
than federal. Uniforms are chosen on the basis of
cut and fabric. And they have punched up the
official motto with the Greenwich Village
Addendum so that it reads as follows: "Neither
snow nor rain nor heat nor gloom of night can
stay these couriers from swift completion of
their appointed rounds. *However*, offended sensibility, painful memory, postman's block, and
previous engagements may stay the courier for
an indefinite period of time. *C'est la vie.*" Closer
examination of this motto reveals these inner
truths:

Offended Sensibility

A Situation of Offended Sensibility is declared
when an assigned route contains the following:
1. Architecture of unpleasant proportion.
2. An excessive number of conceptual artists.
The official definition of "excessive" in such
cases is stated as "More than two if dead,
more than one if alive."
3. Musicians who are awake.

4. Dandyish house pets.
5. Ethnic restaurants featuring interesting food.

Painful Memory

A Situation of Painful Memory can be invoked when a courier is called upon to deliver mail to districts in which:
1. He has had an emotionally satisfactory but physically crippling sexual encounter.
2. He consumed a carelessly prepared shrimp curry.
3. He was snubbed.

Postman's Block

Postman's Block is a virulent condition that attacks the more sensitive couriers with alarming regularity. Its symptoms are:
1. The inability to find the right address caused by an inhibiting perfectionism and a belief that the right address—that big address that you always thought you had in you—shall ever elude your grasp.
2. A tendency to misread zip codes coupled with the nagging doubt that they are perhaps not as zippy as all that.
3. A conviction that you are burnt out. That your great days of swift completion are behind you.

Previous Engagements

The Greenwich Village postman does his best to keep his working hours free but he is, of course, not immune to the killing pace of urban life and frequently discovers that he's booked up pretty solid. This is not surprising since he is a firm believer in the adage "finders keepers" and so is caught up in the dizzying whirl that is the social and business life of others. A look at a page from his appointment calendar reveals the following:

Mardi 6 avril

10:30— Attend board meeting, Ford Foundation
12:00— Conference with agent to discuss Dutch translation
 1:00— Lunch, La Côte Basque—Barbara Walters
 3:30— Address meeting of United Nations Security Council
 6:00— Fashion Show, 500 Club—Stephen Burrows—ready-to-wear
 8:00— Screening at Paramount
10:00— Working dinner—Jonas Salk—Orsini's

Writers on Strike:
A Chilling Prophecy

Major cities are not infrequently afflicted with strikes and demonstrations by doctors, garbage-men, firemen, and police. There is always a public outcry, as those concerned with public safety are quick to envision a city full of burning garbage and contagious murderers. However, garbage in the street, flames in the bedroom, killers on the loose, and spots on the lungs are merely physical inconveniences. Far more serious work stoppages can occur, and politicians and citizens confronted with the more traditional problems can comfort themselves with the thought "Well, it's a hell of a mess but thank God it's not the writers." Because, believe you me, compared to the writers even the Teamsters are a piece of cake.

Imagine, if you will, a rainy Sunday afternoon in New York. All over town, writers are lying in bed, their heads under their respective pillows. They are of varying heights and builds, races, religions, and creeds, but they are as one: whining. Some of them are whining to themselves. Some to companions. It matters not in the least. Simultaneously they all turn over and reach for the phone. In a matter of seconds every

writer in New York is speaking to another writer
in New York. They are talking about not writing.
This is, next to who's not queer, perhaps the
most popular topic of discussion among writers
in New York. Ordinarily there are variations on
this theme and one reacts accordingly:

Variation on This Theme Number One

You can't write. You call another writer. He
can't write, either. This is terrific. You can now
talk about not writing for two hours and then go
out to dinner with each other until four o'clock in
the morning.

Variation on This Theme Number Two

You can't write. You call another writer. He is
writing. *This* is a great tragedy. He will talk to you
only as long as it takes for him to impress upon
you the fact that not only is he writing but he
thinks that *what* he is writing is quite possibly the
best thing he's ever written. Your only alterna-
tive to suicide in this situation is to call a rock
musician. This makes you feel smart again and
you can get on with the business of not writing.

Variation on This Theme Number Three

You are writing. Another writer calls you to

talk about not writing. You announce that you *are*. Masochistically he inquires as to what it is that you are writing. You inform him modestly that it's just a little something vaguely reminiscent of, say, *An Ideal Husband*, perhaps a bit funnier. Your behavior at his funeral the following day is marked by enormous dignity and grace.

There are other variations on this theme but I think you get my drift. Now, on this particular Sunday afternoon a phenomenon has occurred. Every single writer in the city of New York is not writing. Once knowledge of this has spread throughout the entire non-writing writing community, a tremendous feeling of mutual relief and well-being is experienced. For an exquisite moment all the writers in New York like each other. If *no one* can write, then it is obviously not the fault of the writers. It must be *their* fault. The writers band together. They will have their revenge on the city. No longer will they lie abed not writing in the privacy of their own homes. They will not write publicly. They will go on strike. They decide to stage a sitdown in the lobby of the Algonquin Hotel and not write there.

It takes a while but about a year and a half later people begin to notice that there's nothing to read. First they notice that the newsstands are quite empty. Then it begins to get television news coverage. There is still television news, mostly lip sync—some ad lib. People begin to get annoyed. They demand that the city take steps. The city assembles a group to go in and negotiate with the writers. The group consists of a fireman, a doctor, a sanitationman, and a policeman. The writers refuse to negotiate. Their reply to a city on its knees? "Call my agent." The agents refuse to negotiate until they can figure out a way to sell the movie rights. The strike continues. The Red Cross is allowed to cross the picket lines to dispense royalty statements and cappucino. The situation becomes more desperate. Adults all over the country are sitting in bus stations playing jacks. Old copies of *People* magazine are auctioned off and sold at Parke-Bernet for incredible prices. Librarians begin to take bribes and are seen driving lavender Cadillacs with quilted vinyl roofs and page-shaped rear windows. A syndicate is formed by a group who own several back issues of *The New Yorker*. They open a membership-only after-hours reading bar, which is fire-bombed by a radical organization that believes that Donald Barthelme belongs to the people.

Finally the National Guard is called in. Hundreds of heavily armed Guardsmen arrive at the Algonquin. They are forced to retreat under a stinging barrage of sarcastic remarks.

Although the writers have agreed not to have a leader, one of their members becomes something of an authority figure. His influence is based largely on the fact that he has on his person a hardcover copy of *Gravity's Rainbow*, which he is widely believed to have read in its entirety. In reality he is a disguised labor mediator sent by the city to infiltrate the writers and break the strike. He is insidious and stealthily goes about convincing writers that other writers are secretly writing and will have actual manuscripts completed and ready for publication when the strike ends. He does his work well. The writers leave the Algonquin and go back to not writing at home. When they realize they have been duped, and by whom, they are near-suicidal at their lack of perception. So, then, let this be a lesson to you all: never judge a cover by its book.

A Few Words
on a Few Words

Democracy is an interesting, even laudable, notion and there is no question but that when compared to Communism, which is too dull, or Fascism, which is too exciting, it emerges as the most palatable form of government. This is not to say that it is without its drawbacks—chief among them being its regrettable tendency to encourage people in the belief that all men are created equal. And although the vast majority need only take a quick look around the room to see that this is hardly the case, a great many remain utterly convinced.

The major problem resulting from this conviction is that it causes such people to take personally the inalienable right of freedom of speech. This in itself would be at least tolerable were this group not given to such a broad interpretation of the word *freedom* or such a slender interpretation of the word *speech*.

It would further ameliorate the situation were these equality buffs to recall that one of the distinguishing characteristics of democracy is the division between the public sector and the private sector. The founding fathers may have had any number of things in mind when they made this admirable distinction, but surely their primary consideration was to protect the articulate against the possibility of overhearing the annoying conversation of others.

Since the Bill of Rights in its present form leaves far too much to the imagination, it is obviously necessary for some sane, responsible citizen to step forward and explain in detail just exactly what is meant by freedom of speech. Being as civic-minded as the next girl, I willingly accept this challenge. Lest you assume that I possess unreasonable and dangerous dictatorial impulses, I assure you that my desire to curtail undue freedom of speech extends only to such public arenas as restaurants, airports, streets, hotel lobbies, parks, and department stores. Verbal exchanges between consenting adults in private are of as little interest to me as they probably are to them. I wish only to defend the impressionable young and the fastidious old against the ravages of unseemly word usage. To this end I have prepared a list of words which should be used in public only as specified.

    1. *art*—This word may be publicly used in only two instances:
       A. As a nickname—in which case the suffix *ie* may be added to form the word *Artie*.
       B. By a native of the East End of London to describe a vital organ, as in the sentence,

"Blimy, I feel poorly—must be my bleedin' 'art."

2. *love*—The word *love* may be used in public only to refer to inanimate or totally inaccessible objects.

   A. "I love linguini with clam sauce" is always acceptable.

   B. "I love Truman Capote" is acceptable only if one is not personally acquainted with him. If one is personally acquainted with Mr. Capote it is rather unlikely at this time that one would be moved to express such a sentiment.

3. *relationship*—The civilized conversationalist uses this word in public only to describe a seafaring vessel carrying members of his family.

4. *diaphragm*—Public decency demands that this word be used only to refer to the midriff area of the body and then only by doctors—never by singers.

5. *Ms*—The wise avoid this word entirely but:

   A. It may be used on paper by harried members of the publishing world who find it necessary to abbreviate the word manuscript.

   B. Or by native residents of the south and southwestern portions of the United States as follows: "I sho do ms. that purty little gal."

6. *honest*—This word is suitable for public use only to indicate extreme distaste, as in the sentence "Dorothy has become absolutely unbearable—I think she must be on est."

7. *internalize*—To be used (if at all) only to describe that process by which a formerly harmless medical student becomes a menace to the sick and helpless.

8. *fair*—This word is to be used only in reference to a carnival-type event and not as an expression of justice—for not only is such usage unpleasant but also, I assure you, quite useless.

9. *assert*—One would do well to remember that as far as public utterance is concerned, *assert* refers only to that which is two mints in one.

No News Is Preferable

For some it's the columns, for others the logic, but for me when it comes to the most winning aspect of Greek culture I'll take the killing of the bearer of bad news. Throw in the bearer of good news and you've got yourself a practice that's nothing short of perfect. And one, I should like to point out, that would make a welcome addition to any culture, particularly one such as our own. I am, of course, well aware that many people *like* the news—that they consider it to be important, informative, even entertaining. To these people I can only say: You're wrong. Not that I wish to be curt with you—not at all. I am perfectly willing to elaborate. In order that you might more fully understand the error of your ways, let us consider each alleged attribute separately.

Important

When dealing with a concept such as *important* one would be well advised to ask: "To whom?" In this way we can more directly attack the problem. And almost immediately we can see that the "whom" is probably not us. We arrive at this conclusion by asking of ourselves the following questions:

1. Before going to work do I don a highly colored blazer the pocket of which is adorned with a number?
2. Once so attired, do I sit down at a long, curved counter and make jokes with old athletes and minority-group women?
3. Do I periodically interrupt this repartee to look into a camera and relate in an authoritative yet warm tone of voice the unpleasant activities of unattractive people?
4. Do I number among my colleagues at least one who has made a career for herself out of dressing up as a mother and buying dangerous household products?

If our answers to these questions are nos, then I think we can agree that when it comes to the news, "important" is not an appropriate adjective. Unless, of course, you earn your living by delivering papers on a bicycle, in which case the news *is* important but only when compared to you.

Informative

Strictly speaking, the news *is* informative insofar as it does indeed provide information. Therefore the questions one must ask here are:

1. Do I want this information?
2. Do I need this information?
3. What do they expect me to do about it?

Answer to Question Number One

No. If a genetically handicapped Scientologist attempts to take the life of the vice-president of the 4H Clubs of Texas with a crossbow and someone knows about it, I would prefer that he kept it to himself.

Answer to Question Number Two

No. If three unemployed psychopathic black-smiths have stolen the daughter of the inventor of lead paint and are threatening to read to her aloud from *Fear of Flying* until everyone in Marin County is given a horse, I fail to see how knowing this will help me to find a large but inexpensive apartment in a better neighborhood.

Answer to Question Number Three

I cannot possibly imagine.

Entertaining

In researching this subject I watched a fair amount of television news and read a couple of papers. I didn't laugh once.

In the interest of fair play I offer two news situations that I find acceptable. One exists. The other does not. Naturally the one that exists is not nearly as acceptable as the one that does not. And this is probably as good a definition of reality as you are likely to find.

Radio News

Radio news is bearable. This is due to the fact that while the news is being broadcast the disc jockey is not allowed to talk.

Personalized News

Walter Cronkite appears on the screen. He fixes you with a weighty yet good-humored gaze. The whisper of a smile plays around the corners of his forthright mouth. He begins. "Good evening, Fran. While you were lying on the couch today rereading old copies of English *Vogue* and drinking Perrier water your book wrote itself. All indications are that it's perfect. A source close to *The New York Times Book Review* called it 'splendid, brilliantly funny, a surefire hit.' A reputable Hollywood authority—yes, Fran, we found one just for you—reports cutthroat bidding for the movie rights and many in the industry fear that it will set a dangerously high precedent. On the home front, Lauren Bacall called a press conference this afternoon to announce that she wants to trade apartments with you and an informed expert leaked the information that all of the conceptual artists in New York are moving to East Berlin. Well, Fran, that about wraps it up for now. See you tomorrow night, when things will be even better."